THE
COMINTERN
AND
THE SPANISH
CIVIL WAR

Also by E. H. Carr

A HISTORY OF SOVIET RUSSIA
in fourteen volumes

* *with R. W. Davies*

E·H·CARR

THE
COMINTERN
AND
THE SPANISH
CIVIL WAR

EDITED BY

TAMARA DEUTSCHER

PANTHEON BOOKS · NEW YORK

LIBRARY OF CONGRESS CATALOGING IN PUBLICATION DATA

Carr, Edward Hallett, 1892–1982
The Comintern and the Spanish Civil War.

Includes index.
1. Spain—History—Civil War, 1936–1939—Participation, Russian.
2. Communist International—History.
3. Communism—Spain.
4. Russians—Spain—History—20th century.   I. Title.
DP269.47.R8C27   1984   946.081   84-42708
ISBN 0-394-53550-2
ISBN 0-394-72263-9 (pbk.)

Manufactured in the United States of America

First American Edition

CONTENTS

E.H. CARR: A PERSONAL MEMOIR*

In valedictory speeches, and in one or two obituaries of E. H. Carr, the authors – independently of each other – described him as enigmatic. This struck me, and I asked myself why this very English historian seemed so enigmatic to some of his close professional colleagues. In Britain he became, towards the end of his life, something of a monument to scholarship, recognized, admired, if somewhat grudgingly, and a little neglected. But he knew long years of hostility and even ostracism not only by British Academia but also by the Establishment as a whole.

When I first met him, some thirty-six years ago, Carr was in the political and academic wilderness and was just embarking on his great *History of Soviet Russia*. It was at that time that the intellectual friendship between him and Isaac Deutscher was formed. At first sight their personal amity might seem puzzling: on one side, a self-educated former member of the Polish Communist Party – Marxist by conviction, Jewish by origin – who was a refugee from Hitler and Stalin stranded in London; and, on the other side, an English historian who was an unmistakable product of Cambridge, a former member of the Foreign Office, schooled in a diplomatic service famous as a bastion of British traditionalism. But they were both under attack (if an attack veiled by formal respect), and both were debarred from academic posts. They were also both engaged in the study of the Soviet Union – albeit from two quite different angles: one a historian of institutions and policies, increasingly under Marxist influence; the other an unrepentant Marxist, analysing movements and ideas, surveying a society in turmoil torn by ideological battles. The "enigma" of that friendship, and of the personality of Carr himself, becomes perhaps less perplexing once one understands the degree to which Carr was *in* the British tradition and yet was not quite *of* it; the extent to which he was an intellectual expatriate from the world of diplomacy, a rebel against his own tradition, criticizing it – as it were – from within.

* Reprinted from *New Left Review*, No. 137, Jan.–Feb. 1983.

When the two men first got to know each other, the cold war was just closing in. Carr had the reputation of having been an "appeaser" before the war, and then a "fellow-traveller" during or after it – a stigma that was, of course, a politically much more serious one at the time. It was true that, carried away by indignation against the injustices and stupidities of the Versailles settlement, he had seen Germany for long – for too long – as nothing but a defenceless victim of that settlement, and had tended to view Hitler as a run-of-the-mill statesman in revolt against it. His diplomatic training predisposed him to concentrate his attention on the state rather than to observe society, and he did not perceive the degree to which German society became degraded and corrupted by Fascism. Not until 1938 did he become alerted to the dangers which Hitler's ideology and militarism presented to Europe and the world. Too much of a realist not to be aware that British antagonism to both Germany and Russia was untenable, he then turned his eyes towards the Soviet Union – which had already aroused his interest in the early 1920s. The spectacle of the Stalinist purges of 1936–1938 may have been revolting to him, but it became somewhat blurred by the undoubted economic achievements of the USSR and by the Five Year Plans which seemed to deal so effectively with the anarchy of capitalism in crisis in the West. With Russian entry into the war, the might of the Red Army could not but impress and inspire the admiration of the ex-diplomat who still remembered the sorry sight of Russia on the morrow of the First World War. Now the Soviet Union was, and would remain, an ally whose blemishes could be disregarded or excused. It was respectable to discount these while the brunt of the fighting was borne by the Russian armies in the East. But when the cease-fire sounded and our gallant ally became the villain of the peace, those who opposed the reversal of alliances were derided as fellow-travellers; and as the cold war intensified, this label became more and more damaging. Hence the isolation in which Carr started on his immense work on the USSR in these years.

OUTSIDE THE "CHARMED CIRCLE"

What eventually turned the young diplomat into the famous historian of the Soviet Union? The origins of his interest in the outcome of the October Revolution went back to his early days in the Foreign Office; for, according to his own account, it was the Revolution which decisively gave him a sense of history. By a "lucky hunch", and also from his *esprit de contradiction*, he was one of those exceptional British diplomats who right from the beginning did not think the Petersburg upheaval was a flash in the pan, but believed that the Bolsheviks had come to stay. He regarded the Western reaction to this prospect as – I quote from an unpublished autobiographical memoir – "narrow, blind, and stupid". "I had some vague impression of the revolutionary views of Lenin and Trotsky, but knew nothing of Marxism; I had probably never heard of Marx."

It was, however, nineteenth-century Russian literature which presented him with an ideological challenge at this time. Reading Dostoevsky, Herzen and others, he perceived for the first time "that the liberal moralistic ideology in which I had been brought up was not, as I had always assumed, an Absolute taken for granted by the modern world, but was sharply and convincingly attacked by very intelligent people living outside the charmed circle, who looked at the world through very different eyes.... This left me in a very confused state of mind: I reacted more and more sharply against the Western ideology, but still from a point somehow within it. (Perhaps I have never quite escaped from this dilemma.)"

This consciousness of belonging to the "charmed circle", yet seeing the world through different eyes, of being at once part of it and rebelling against it, increased the sense of isolation which had pursued Carr since his youth. He was, as he used to say, a "clever boy" and never doubted his ability to come out top of the class. But "boys who always come top of the class aren't very popular with their schoolmates. This may have been one of the causes of a certain sense of 'isolation'." "I think I never lost the sense of not fitting easily into my environment", he confessed. This feeling of distance was masked later in life by a kind of Olympian detachment which many took for intellectual arrogance.

I met Carr in 1946 or 1947. After Isaac's death in 1967 we maintained very friendly though more distant relations. It was during the last decade of his life that we became closely associated. For in 1972, after some preliminary meetings and correspondence, he wrote a letter to me which was in fact an appeal for help. He was then engaged on what should have been the last volume of his *History*, dealing with international relations in the period 1926–1929. The book "seemed to grow" in his hands. To give me some idea of his work, he enclosed a plan of the whole volume: it looked formidably daunting to me. Apart from dealing with "diplomatic coexistence" between East and West, it also contained developments within Western communist parties; another chapter, "World Revolution", was devoted to the Comintern, Profintern, and the "machinery" of these institutions (including something cryptically called "statistics"); then followed a long list of more exotic topics about which I knew nothing: Turkey, Egypt, Afghanistan, Outer Mongolia, China, Indonesia, the Negro Question, etc.

"The amount of material which I ought to consult is enormous", he wrote, "and I sometimes get oppressed – and depressed – with the idea that I shall never be able to finish. . . . Will you help me?" What was I to do except plead ignorance? How was I to help? He was somewhat vague: "I won't attempt to define exactly what I need because I need whatever you can give me – searching for material in the British Museum, in the LSE, . . . perhaps in the University Library here which has a few things." Then, to be more persuasive, the letter resorted to an outsized dose of flattery: we should be "meeting and talking over my drafts and criticizing and correcting them. It would be a relief to have somebody to consult, and feel I was not working entirely alone. Nobody could do this for me except you." More convincing were his other arguments: it was true that the job I had left a few months before was silly and boring, and searching for material and discussing his drafts would be immeasurably more stimulating. "I know that you also found your previous job tiring – with me you could at least be able to work as much or as little as you wanted and when you wanted; there would be no timetable." All this was, of course, extremely attractive, though ill-defined.

The letter was also a very moving one: "Now that I've summoned up courage, I'm impatient for an answer – but only if it's the right one!" There was something appealing in this suggestion of helplessness in a man who loomed so large as a power on the international intellectual horizon. "I am so anxious about the future of my work." "I don't know how we can work together, but I'm sure we can." To my relief, the letter ended on a very matter-of-fact note: "Have you got dates of Trotsky's correspondence with Preobrazhensky and Rakovsky about China?" It was easier to find an answer to this question than to know exactly "how we can work together".

In his scheme of things he would need my help for a year or so, just the time needed to finish the final, twelfth volume of his monumental *History*. The "last" volume grew into three, and when the complete boxed edition of the *magnum opus* appeared, it carried the story down to the end of 1929 and consisted of fourteen quite bulky volumes. The impact it has made on the international concourse of "Sovietology" is well known. The Soviet journals themselves mention it critically, their usual formula being that "even-the-bourgeois-historian Carr" knows something about the USSR; the Chinese straightaway bought forty copies of the whole set.

Long before the celebratory lunch given by the publisher on the occasion of the completion of this immense work, various files on Carr's desk contained random notes on his future labours. "Well," he said to me, "you see I have to keep myself occupied." He allowed himself, however, a respite which took the form of writing with breathtaking speed *The Russian Revolution from Lenin to Stalin, 1917–1929*. All the fourteen volumes over which he had laboured for thirty years were so fresh in his mind, that it took him no more than a few weeks to "distil" them into two hundred pages of "a new composition in which scarcely a sentence from the original work reappears unchanged". He also "kept himself busy" preparing a collection of his essays which had appeared mainly in *The Times Literary Supplement* since the 1950s. These preoccupations he termed "somewhat frivolous", a word which he liked very much and which denoted for him something lighthearted and pleasurable. (*The Romantic Exiles* had been, he said, written "in a frivolous mood".*) Simultaneously, he was giving more and more attention to the material which went into the making of *The Twilight of Comintern* (published a few weeks after his death).

WORKING WITH CARR

Now, five or six books and ten years later, I still recall the

---

* Only years later I noticed that he had slipped the following note into the volume of *The Romantic Exiles* which he gave me at Christmas 1972: "Some of this needs to be read with indulgence. I was still terribly young at 40."

bewilderment and uncertainty with which at first I faced the vague prospect of "working together". As "it wouldn't be fair" that I should always travel to him, he proposed fortnightly meetings of two days alternately in his home and in mine. I was wondering how uncomfortable at his age he might feel in my – by his standards – somewhat bohemian, unstaffed and unregulated, household. It was amazing how easily he adapted to minor disturbances to which he was not accustomed. Even a major catastrophe like a leaking ceiling in his bedroom during a night of torrential rain did not seem to affect his capacity for work next morning. A breakdown of central heating, a radio blaring on the building site outside the window, telephone calls or tradesmen at the door at the most inconvenient moment in the middle of a discussion – nothing seemed to distract him or impair his serenity. Yet he was in no way above ordinary day-to-day concerns: he always exchanged a few words with my domestic help, remembered the name of her daughter, pointed out the merits or demerits of a gardener, reminded me that the name of the man who had a year before mended the roof was Mr Murphy not Mr Miller (although he had heard the name only once). He was intensely interested in the doings – public and private – of my friends, especially the much younger ones, and even of their children. (Press notices of Susie's or Pauline's concerts were promptly dispatched to me from Cambridge.)

Ensconced in his favourite armchair, with a great number of little notes spread on the floor and coffee tables around him, he would go on writing quickly and fluently, undisturbed by interruptions and outside noises. His method of work presented some difficulties for me. His very first draft of any chapter was barely ten pages long. This is what I know, he would say. Then started the process of "filling the gaps": a first list of questions would appear and we would discuss where I could find at least some of the answers. Where were the original sources? Were they available in this country? Could we get something from Harvard? From Feltrinelli? Who were the authors who also dealt with the topic? – And so on.

On the basis of his research and mine, he would then try to "fill the gaps" by writing insertions: pages additional to his first draft. These insertions were, of course, of various lengths. One then had to "insert" new material into the first set of "insertions": these were mostly slips of flimsy paper of all shapes and sizes with old notes or letters on the reverse, covered with tiny handwriting in pen or pencil, all precariously pinned together. This, of course, played havoc with any attempt to number the pages consecutively. Such was, however, the lucidity of his composition that even when some insertion slips went astray or were temporarily "lost", it was easy to find their place in the tightly knit narrative. In this way, the initial draft of ten pages or so would grow into a considerable text perhaps ten times the original length. Only one typist, in far-away Scotland, who worked for him for the last twenty-five years of his life, could decipher Ted Carr's manuscript. The typed text would be returned to us for further revision – there were, of course, more gaps to be filled, more questions to be answered, and more insertions pinned on.

What also made my task a complicated one was his incredible ability to work on different parts of the book simultaneously: just when I was trying to grapple with what was supposed to be Ch'en Tu-hsiu's reports to the Central Committee of the Chinese Party in the summer of 1926, a note would arrive from Cambridge: Carr had just found that he did not have enough details about the reaction of certain Italians to the expulsion of Tasca from the PCI in 1929. At such moments I was glad indeed that, as he had said in his original letter, he "could no longer work long hours or very fast".

All these were, however, difficulties of a technical character and could be overcome with a little flexibility on both sides. Not so "technical" were the difficulties which stemmed from our different approaches to historiography. Brought up in quite a different school in these matters, I was somewhat impatient with what I saw as his excessive preoccupation with constitutions, resolutions, formal programmes, official pronouncements, and so on. I thought that as these were typically all more honoured in the breach than observed in practice, it was not essential to pay so much attention to them. It seemed to me that he was attaching too much weight to the letter and perhaps not enough to the spirit of his documentation.

He would listen to my objections with patience, benevolence and an indulgent smile. Since he was "addicted to the minutiae of precision and accuracy" – the words are his – he would challenge me to substantiate my objections. But we both knew that "the spirit" is always by its nature so much more difficult to "document". He would want me to produce a quotable proof of something as elusive as a "ferment of ideas" or a malaise permeating one or another communist party. But while it was a simple matter to read diligently through sets of *Humanité* or *Pravda* and make copious notes from them, it was not so simple to ascertain the state of mind of those former contributors to them – writers or party activists – whose names at some point disappeared from their pages. It was one thing to summarize the substance of the speeches made at party congresses, and quite another to attempt to convey the mood of those who were expelled or debarred. True, there was usually a certain amount of political literature produced by a variety of oppositions, but it was normally not abundant nor easy to come by. The "subversive" ideas of a minority, especially of a defeated minority, are never as well documented as those of a victorious establishment. To do full justice to these ideas required imagination and empathy.

Such were the few small difficulties of working with Carr. Immeasurably greater, however, was the satisfaction, the intellectual excitement and enrichment, that I derived from our essentially harmonious cooperation. When in my home we would stop work at about six. While I would still be ruminating – in the kitchen – over Stalin's "Letter to *Proletarskaya Revolyutsiya*" or the dullness of a speech by Kuusinen, Carr would be resting. After supper we would listen to music, which was for him the best form of relaxation. He would choose a record: nearly always Beethoven, Mozart or Schubert. Although he never played an instrument himself, he was knowledgeable about music and had an amazing memory for it. He was delighted when the BBC invited him to be a guest on its record programme *Man of Action*. This was a pleasurably "frivolous" distraction.

In the evenings we hardly ever discussed problems of current work. Political topics of the day were not too welcome either, though they were not barred. What was barred were all "fundamental" philosophical discussions. He had a horror of the kind of long debates to which so many of his nineteenth-century Slavonic heroes were conspicuously addicted. He had, he said, a very long time ago settled in his own mind, once and for all, the problems of Absolutes, of Basic Principles, of Morality and Conscience, of Human Nature, and of the "Meaning of Life". Any kind of philosophical terminology jarred on him and he would quickly put away in the farthest corner of the room any book which smacked to him of such jargon. With (mock?) humility, he never tired of insisting that he had no ability for abstract thinking. Any fleeting influence that the philosophy of Russell or Moore may have had on him during his student days at Cambridge, when he "first heard the name of Hegel", he dismissed lightly. But he was proud of the "flair for cutting through a load of nonsense and getting straight to the point" which he said he had learned as a classicist from A. E. Housman, whom he considered to possess "the most powerful intellectual machinery" he had "ever seen in action".

THE "AMATEUR" MARXIST

This gift for getting straight to the point enabled him to evaluate great masses of historical material very quickly, as well as to follow much contemporary historiographical and political literature. What could seem like a superficial scanning of pages gave him quite a precise idea of what was enclosed between the covers of a book. I often watched how he dealt, for example, with works submitted for the annual Deutscher Prize: within one morning he would glance at several such works, read extremely rapidly a chapter here and a fragment there, make a few notes and then produce a succinct and precise report summing up their contents and detailing his opinions of them. He had a marked preference for empirical over theoretical or "abstract" materials. Also a preference for young writers. One characteristic comment runs: "I am very much an amateur Marxist, and soon get out of my depth. Also I may have a hidden preference for the English idiom in which I grew up, over the German-American."

Was he a Marxist — be it an "amateur" Marxist? Was he a socialist? In time, scholarly doctorates will no doubt be written proving or disproving his socialism or his Marxism. During his informal talks with me he seemed essentially a nineteenth-century liberal who had become exceedingly impatient with the anarchy of modern capitalism. For his original liberal faith did not survive the practical abandonment of free trade, the cornerstone of his political upbringing. But although in consequence he quite early became convinced of the "bankruptcy of capitalism", "it would be fair to say that I have always been more interested in Marxism as a method of revealing the hidden springs of thought and action, and debunking the logical and moralistic façade generally erected around them, than in the Marxist analysis of the decline of capitalism. Capitalism was clearly on the way out, and the precise mechanism of its downfall did not seem to me all that interesting." He would say that he was not a Marxist only in so far as he "could not see the Western proletariat, the progeny of Western bourgeois capitalism, as the bearer of world revolution in its next stage".

Surveying the contemporary political scene shortly before his death, he expressed his exasperation in a brief sentence which is intelligible enough: "The Left is foolish and the Right is vicious." He was no reformist and did not believe that socialism could be attained through the machinery of bourgeois democracy, but he also deplored as an illusion the idea that the working class would in the foreseeable future be either able or willing to fight for socialism. He saw the labour movement in full retreat and was impatient with what he took to be the "New Left" and its "theorizing about a revolutionary situation without enquiring whether it exists". The "unity of theory and practice", he remarked, "cuts both ways". In the late 1970s, he was "shattered" – the word is his – by what he saw as the political naiveté of much of the European Left.

Eurocommunism was to him a doctrine which "had no leg to stand on", but was making its own contribution to the outbreak of the new cold war. So, to his mind, was any excessive or uncritical preoccupation with the Soviet dissidents. On this he expressed himself with unusual sharpness in a letter: "What can one think of 'Eurocommunists' who have produced no programme of their own, but are prepared at the drop of a hat to rub shoulders with declared counter-revolutionaries (anti-Lenin, anti-Marx) and cold warriors? This must be meat and drink to hardliners in the Kremlin. Back to the 'united front from Trotsky to Chamberlain'? At least Trotsky never did that." "Where are we going? There are too many war-mongers around the world at present for comfort. Cannot the New Left go back to Nuclear Disarmament? Also perhaps a bit naive, but healthier."

This kind of outburst was, however, very rare, and I suspect that it may have been brought on by a general irritation with the difficulties of his daily life and his sense of failing strength. "It's depressing to reflect how much more quickly, and with how much less effort I used to work" – this was becoming now, when he was well into his ninth decade, an oft-repeated refrain. He was painfully aware that he had no more than a few years in front of him, and he was very anxious about the future of his work.

As time went on, remembrance of things past loomed larger and larger in our evening conversations. But unlike many old men, he was not *difficilis, querulus, laudator temporis acti*. Nor was he a critic or censor of the new generation. On the contrary, he was attracted by the young and felt at ease with those fifty or sixty years his juniors. He was enthusiastic about the admission of women to his college – a measure long overdue in his judgement. Unlike some of his academic colleagues, and unlike the stewards, porters and waiters of the college, he was not at all shocked by the appearance of the long-haired young fellows and dons in jeans and shirtsleeves at the high table. He thought the young were neither more nor less "moral" or "serious" than they had been in his days, and all bemoaning of "our permissive society" he treated as nothing but cant.

In his reminiscences he used to go back to his pre-1914 past. His very short and cramped autobiographical sketch, written less than a year ago, begins thus: "'Security' is the first word which occurs to me if I look back on my youth – security . . . in a sense scarcely imaginable since 1914." That year was the end of an epoch; since then Europe and the world have been plunged into a turmoil which to him was becoming increasingly frightening. Yet he fought against any mood of pessimism and gloom, and did not share any apocalyptic vision of the future. The remnants of his nineteenth-century liberal optimism were still with him, and continued to nourish utopian longings.

Yes, the man so often described as a *Realpolitiker par excellence* had his Utopia. It was a vague, undefined Utopia but, as he wrote, "I suppose I should call it 'socialist'". This in no way excluded a nostalgia for the past which he perhaps expressed best in an amusing note he sent me on August 9, 1982: "80th anniversary of the Coronation of King Edward VII, postponed from June for the removal of his appendix. I was on a family holiday at Exmouth, and remember the decorations and fireworks. Why could we not go on living forever and ever in that innocent world?"

London, November 1982   TAMARA DEUTSCHER

INTRODUCTION

This volume has been published posthumously. When E. H. Carr died, on November 3, 1982, at the age of 90, he left the manuscript practically finished, though not quite ready for the printer.

To those familiar with E. H. Carr's monumental *History* and his other work, it will come as no surprise to learn that the author intended to carry the story of the relations between the Comintern and most, if not all, of its "Sections" right through to 1943, the year of its final dissolution; he had prepared a great deal of material on this. For a time he even thought of devoting his labours to the history of the war years as well as the immediate postwar period. This was to follow *The Twilight of Comintern, 1930–1935* which appeared in December 1982, and of which the author had the satisfaction of seeing the first available advance copy.

The Twilight of Comintern ends with the year 1935 and the seventh congress called, after considerable delay, seven years after the previous one in 1928. Although the seventh congress elected an Executive Committee charged with the preparation of the next gathering at some future date, in fact it was the last. The eighth congress never took place. Thus the institution originally designed as the General Staff of the future world revolution faded out when the proletariat was facing the mortal danger of counter-revolution throughout Europe.

Towards the end of the ninth decade of his long and productive life, E. H. Carr felt somewhat overwhelmed by the magnitude of the task he had set himself. He found it increasingly difficult to scrutinize with his usual punctiliousness the wealth of documentary material available for this, the most stormy period of contemporary history, and became more and more painfully aware that he might be obliged to limit the scope of his research and writing. Initially, the story of the Comintern and the Spanish civil war was to form only one chapter of the immense *oeuvre*, but some time in 1981 he decided, reluctantly, to concentrate his waning strength on this fragment of history. What reconciled him to the change of plan was the recognition that the Spanish civil war deserved more detailed treatment, as both the dress rehearsal for and the prelude to the approaching Great Contest. He was swayed, too, by the availability of new material, mainly the publication of Palmiro Togliatti's confidential reports sent from Spain to the headquarters of the Communist International in Moscow.

But it is not any new documentation which makes this book an invaluable addition to the existing literature on the Spanish civil war and the Comintern. Its great merit is that the author provides us with a new perspective on the complexity of the motives which lay behind Stalin's policy and on the intricate relationship of forces in Europe of that period. The historian of the Soviet regime demonstrates, with his usual lucidity, how it came about that Moscow's attitude to Spain was dictated less and less by the *raison de la révolution* and more and more by the Soviet *raison d'état*. In the previous volume E. H. Carr dealt with the twilight of Comintern; in this, he shows how completely and irreversibly in this "twilit world...substance melted into shadow". And the shadow was ominous: together with genuine military instructors and advisers, Stalin dispatched to Spain also the agents of his political police, and exported the internecine struggle from Moscow to war-torn Madrid, Barcelona and Valencia.

Carr was not only the historian of the Russian Revolution; he was also an exceptionally astute analyst of the policies of Western democracies. His years in the corridors of diplomacy and his cool detachment allowed him to see with extraordinary clarity the extent to which, behind all the diplomatic manoeuvrings, there loomed the old ideological antagonism. To France and Britain, Stalin remained the fomenter of revolution, no matter how "moderate", "democratic" and "patriotic" his Popular Front slogans were. To some European socialists, he looked more and more like a gravedigger of the revolution. To Stalin, the policy of appeasement which culminated in the Munich agreement seemed due not to the short-sightedness or weakness of Western govern-ments, but to their inveterate fear of communism, and, he suspected, to the wish to deflect the might of the Axis onto the East.

Carr, with his sharp mind and what he sometimes referred to as his "flair for cutting through a load of nonsense", exposes the hollowness of the moral indignation at Fascist aggression expressed by politicians in Paris and London, and at the Geneva conventicles. Their inactivity dressed up as a high-sounding "principle of non-intervention" degenerated into cruel farce and, in fact, left defenceless Spain to fight alone the first battle of the Second World War.

The most intractable material is here woven into a narrative even more close-textured than in the author's previous books. Had he lived longer, he would have revised it and reworked it further. He wrote with a sense of swiftly passing time, and this underlying haste seems to heighten the intensity of the story as it moves to its tragic conclusion, and conveys all the more poignantly the magnitude of the disaster which befell Spain, and Europe.

E. H. Carr was generous in acknowledging, in the prefaces to his successive volumes, his indebtedness to many scholars, institutions and friends who helped him in his labours. It is a matter of pride that he entrusted the final editing of the manuscript to me. He rightly foresaw that in this the cooperation of Jonathan Haslam, who had assisted him throughout the writing of this volume, would prove invaluable. He had also encouraged me to take advantage of the knowledge and experience of Professor R. W. Davies, the co-author of the first two volumes of *Foundations of a Planned Economy* (1969). I should like to express my gratitude to both scholars, without whose help and expertise my task would have been more difficult. My personal thanks go to Mr John H. Carr for his trust, support and affection.

London, June 1983   TAMARA DEUTSCHER

LIST OF ABBREVIATIONS

CEDA	=	Confederación Española de Derechas Autónomas (Spanish Confederation of Autonomous Right-wing Groups)
CGT	=	Confédération Générale du Travail
CGTU	=	Confederación General del Trabajo Unitaria
	=	Confédération Générale du Travail Unitaire
CNT	=	Confederación Nacional del Trabajo (Anarchist)
Comintern	=	Communist International
CPGB	=	Communist Party of Great Britain
FAI	=	Federación Anarquista Ibérica (Iberian Anarchist Federation)
FNTT	=	Federación Nacional de Trabajadores de la Tierra (Agricultural Section of the UGT)
IKKI	=	Ispolnitel'nyi Komitet Kommunisticheskogo Internatsionala (Executive Committee of the Communist International [Comintern])
ILP	=	Independent Labour Party
KPP	=	Komunistyczna Partja Polski (Polish Communist Party)
LSI	=	Labour and Socialist International – Second International
Narkomindel	=	Narodnyi Komissariat Inostrannykh Del (People's Commissariat of Foreign Affairs)
NKVD	=	Narodnyi Komissariat Vnutrennykh Del (People's Commissariat of Internal Affairs)
PCE	=	Partido Comunista de España
PCF	=	Parti Communiste Français
PCI	=	Partito Comunista Italiano
POUM	=	Partido Obrero de Unificación Marxista (Marxist Workers' Unity Party)
PSOE	=	Partido Socialista Obrero Español
PSUC	=	Partido Socialista Unificado de Cataluña
Second International	=	Labour and Socialist International
SFIO	=	Section Française Internationale Ouvrière (French Socialist Party)
SIM	=	Servicio de Investigación Militar
TUC	=	Trade Union Congress
UGT	=	Union General de Trabajadores (General Union of Workers [Socialist])

THE
COMINTERN
AND
THE SPANISH
CIVIL WAR

1
THE PRELUDE

The Spanish Communist Party (PCE) greeted the decisions of the seventh congress of Comintern with unalloyed enthusiasm.[1] The change of line at the congress, which had not only enjoined cooperation between communists and socialists in a united front, but had envisaged a broad popular anti-Fascist alliance, gave it the first opportunity to enter effectively the troubled arena of Spanish politics. Its eagerness to contribute to the consolidation of the anti-Fascist popular front in its broadest form (Bloque Popular as distinguished from Frente Unico) was demonstrated by its participation on October 20, 1935, in a public meeting organized by the Left Republican Party and addressed by its leader, Azaña.[2] The strength of the anarchist trade union federation (CNT) made it everywhere a formidable rival of the socialist UGT: in some areas, notably in Catalonia and Aragon, the CNT and its political wing (FAI) dominated the forces of the Left. This situation, peculiar to Spain, rendered the socialists more amenable than elsewhere to cooperation with the communists.

Unfortunately, however, advances from the PCE had the effect of aggravating fissiparous tendencies in the Spanish Socialist Workers' Party (PSOE), which ever since 1931 had wrestled unsuccessfully with the problem of whether to support, or to denounce, the bourgeois republic. While the former Right of the PSOE, with its leader Besteiro, was discredited, the party was now divided between a moderate centre led by Prieto and a revolutionary wing led by the flamboyant Largo Caballero, a forceful trade union leader, recently released from prison. Each group had its weekly journal, *Claridad* being the organ of Largo Caballero, and *El Socialista*, the official party organ, representing the moderates. The two groups, already at odds on

[1] J. Díaz, *Tres Años de Lucha* (Paris, 1970), pp. 31–57, *Rundschau*, No. 7, February 13, 1936, pp. 276–277. For the earlier history of the PCE see *The Twilight of Comintern, 1930–1935* (1982), pp. 289–318.

[2] *Rundschau*, No. 59, October 24, 1935, p. 2420.

questions of social policy, split decisively on the specific issue of the popular front, which in the broad form proposed by the PCE appealed to neither group, Prieto desiring a coalition with the bourgeois radical republicans to the exclusion of the PCE, and Largo Caballero a workers' united front of the PSOE and the PCE, free from any taint of an alliance with the bourgeoisie. On October 23, 1935, the central committee of the PCE addressed an open letter to *Claridad* which went far to accept Largo Caballero's programme. It called for trade union unity through the incorporation of the communist CGTU in the socialist UGT, for the formation of an anti-Fascist popular bloc on the basis of the proletarian united front, and for the "organic political unity of the proletariat", implying "full independence *vis-à-vis* the bourgeoisie, and a complete break-up of the social-democratic bloc with the bourgeoisie". The letter ended by citing the principle of democratic centralism and the example of the Russian Bolsheviks.[3]

Largo Caballero's rejection of cooperation with bourgeois radical republicans, and the apparent readiness of the PCE to fall in with his views, not only aggravated the divisions in the PSOE, but threatened the whole conception of a broad popular anti-Fascist front. It caused bewilderment and anxiety in Comintern. Early in November 1935, Duclos, the PCF leader who had previously worked as Comintern delegate in Spain,[4] was despatched to Madrid in an attempt to clear up this hitch in the policy of the popular front. Largo Caballero was both vain and stubborn. Having occupied himself in prison with reading the works of Marx and Lenin, he saw himself as the great leader of the Spanish revolution,[5] and did not respond favourably to discouraging signals from Moscow. After three days of arduous discussion between him and Duclos, some sort of agreement seems to have been patched up, and Duclos returned to Paris, and thence to Moscow, to report.[6] Such restraint as was shown by Largo

---

[3] *Ibid*. No. 63, November 7, 1935, pp. 2524–2525.

[4] See *The Twilight of Comintern, 1930–1935* (1982), pp. 292–293, 303.

[5] The precedent of Russia in 1917 was frequently invoked – and not only by communists – in the Spain of 1935. Largo Caballero was reported as having said to an American journalist: "Lenin declared that Spain would be the second Soviet republic in Europe. Lenin's prophecy will come true. I shall be the second Lenin who will make it come true." He later denied the report as a libel; but the phrase "the second Lenin" stuck (D. Cattell, *Communism and the Spanish Civil War* [1965], p. 220, note 5).

[6] J. Duclos, *Mémoires*, ii (1969), 109–111.

Caballero in subsequent proceedings was probably due not so much to the persuasive arguments of Duclos as to the hard fact that, while the communists were responsible for the slogan of the popular front, and Largo Caballero for its most resounding oratory, the voting strength of the PSOE in most parts of Spain remained predominantly on the side of Prieto and the moderates.

To organize the popular front for the electoral struggle was now an urgent task. The Cortes, having failed to give their confidence to any workable government, were dissolved early in January 1936, and new elections announced for February 16. On January 15 agreement was reached between Left republicans, the PSOE, the PCE, and apparently some anarchists, on a programme which constituted the electoral platform of the front. It called for the release of political prisoners, and the reinstatement of those who had been removed from their posts by the "Fascist regime" after the rising of October 1934, for financial and fiscal reforms, and for the reform of the judiciary. Perhaps the most remarkable feature of the programme was the absence of any serious social and economic demands. Agitation for the taking over of the land by peasants and of factories by the workers was actively pursued by the Left and supported by the UGT and its land-workers' section (FNTT). But this was not reflected or encouraged in the programme of the popular front. In terms of the heated controversies of the day, it was a mild and anodyne document, evidently designed to rally a wide coalition of divergent interests and sectors of opinion, united only in their commitment to the republic and to some form of democratic government.[7] But for the moment it served its purpose. Díaz's pre-election speeches, tactfully addressed to "Workers and Anti-Fascist Comrades", were an impassioned plea for the popular front and the defence of Spanish democracy.[8] The elections to the Cortes on February 16, 1936, were a victory for the popular front, with 278 deputies, including 88 socialists and 16 communists; PCE candidates received in all 400,000 votes. The anarchists, true to their principles, put forward no candidates of their own. But some anarchists appear to have voted for popular front candidates. The Centre parties, with only 67 deputies, were the heaviest losers. The Right had 140 deputies, of whom 94 were

[7] *Rundschau*, No. 4, January 23, 1936, pp. 142–143.

[8] J. Díaz, *Tres Años de Lucha* (Paris, 1970), pp. 61–98; they included a much applauded personal eulogy of Largo Caballero (p. 87), as well as an appeal to the anarchists to join the front (p. 89).

members of the Confederacíon Española de Derechas Autonómas (CEDA), the Catholic quasi-Fascist party led by Gil Robles.[9]

The elections were followed by an amnesty; and the release of 30,000 political prisoners, held for alleged complicity in the rising of October 1934, was greeted with scenes of popular enthusiasm. *Pravda* hailed the "polarization of class forces", but recognized that the forces of reaction and Fascism had not been destroyed, and could be overcome only by a popular front leading to "the creation of a unified revolutionary party of the proletariat".[10] Nevertheless, it was the first victory of a popular front government in Europe. Díaz, in a carefully worded statement, called for a further strengthening of the popular bloc. Unity of action between communists, socialists and anarchists through the worker and peasant alliances must be extended "in a linkage with the Left republicans and democratic masses", the ultimate aim being fusion of the CNT with the UGT.[11] The theme of unity was in the air. In France, the rival socialist and communist trade union federations, the CGT and the CGTU, with the blessing of Comintern, were about to consummate their union at the Toulouse congress of March 5–7, 1936.[12] Togliatti, writing in the Russian party journal, hailed the Spanish elections as "an event which acquires enormous significance, nationally and internationally", and "a splendid victory in the struggle for the unity of the proletariat against Fascism". The influence of the PCE was not yet decisive. But the lessons of the need for unity had been learned: "in no other country have the decisions of the seventh congress had such vast and profound effects".[13]

Electoral victory thus stimulated the demand for closer union in the ranks of the Left. On March 4, 1936, the central committee of the PCE addressed the PSOE with a proposal for the constitution of joint socialist–communist worker and peasant groups at all levels from local to national: the ultimate aim was to be a "worker–peasant government" based on these groups – the

[9] For detailed figures of the parties, with gains and losses, see *Rundschau*, No. 14, March 26, 1936, p. 583.

[10] *Pravda*, February 19, 1936.

[11] *Rundschau*, No. 10, February 27, 1936, p. 371; J. Díaz, *Tres Años de Lucha* (Paris, 1970) pp. 88–89.

[12] March 1936 was also the month of the famous interview with the American journalist Roy Howard, in which Stalin described the attribution to the USSR of projects of world revolution as a "tragi-comic misunderstanding".

[13] *Bol'shevik*, No. 6, March 15, 1936, pp. 9–19.

Spanish equivalent of a government of Soviets.[14] On March 26, 1936, the executive committees of the youth leagues of the PCE and PSOE met in Madrid, and announced their intention to create "an organization of a new kind", said to be based on the decisions of the sixth congress of KIM in Moscow in the previous September – the sequel of the seventh congress of Comintern a month earlier; the proclamation invoked the names of Largo Caballero and Dimitrov, and also appealed to anarchist youth to "take its place in the struggle for the unity of revolutionary youth". A further document appealed to all members of the communist and socialist youth organizations to unite their forces, and announced the formation of a joint commission to prepare for a unification congress of the two leagues.[15] The campaign for trade union unity progressed more slowly. At a congress of the CNT in Saragossa in May 1936, a majority of the delegates voted for unity with the UGT, but at the same time insisted on an all-out revolutionary programme and no compromises with supporters of the bourgeois republic.[16] Once these aims were revealed as incompatible, a split was bound to follow.

A session of an "enlarged" central committee of the PCE in Madrid on March 28-30, 1936, was attended by delegates from all the provinces of Spain, and from the autonomous communist parties of Catalonia and the Basque regions. Its main concern, at the moment of the triumph of the Left, was to uphold the revolutionary image of the party. Electoral victory had been characterized "not only by the powerful political awakening of the workers and peasants, but by the profound radicalization of the middle strata". The PCE must address itself to "the pressing task of the organization of the revolution", and to "the realization of political unity through the creation of a single Marxist–Leninist party". The party now claimed a membership of 50,000.[17] Díaz

[14] The PCE communication was published in *Claridad*, March 12, 1936, but appears to have received no formal answer.

[15] *Rundschau*, No. 17, April 16, 1936, pp. 691–692; according to Díaz (*ibid*. No. 20, April 30, 1936, p. 809), otherwise unrecorded conversations in Moscow in March 1936 between Spanish socialist and communist youth delegates and Manuilsky and Dimitrov played an important part in promoting the agreement.

[16] *Rundschau*, No. 23, May 14, 1936, p. 932; for an account of the congress see S. Payne, *The Spanish Revolution* (1970), pp. 199–201.

[17] *Rundschau*, No. 16, April 8, 1936, p. 651; No. 23, May 14, 1936, pp. 921–923; according to another account, membership is said to have risen from 30,000 in February 1936 to 100,000 in June (*Pod Znamenem Ispanskoi Respubliki* [1965], p. 435, note 69).

devoted his first major speech in the Cortes on behalf of the PCE on April 15 to a slashing attack on the Right and to a plea for the programme of the popular front, which he summarized as "democracy, freedom, welfare and peace".[18] The party was strengthened at this time by the return to Spain of a group of 79 refugees who had fled to the USSR after the failure of the Asturias rising of October 1934, and had remained there ever since. The group announced its departure from Moscow in widely publicized letters of April 5, 1936, to Dimitrov and Stalin, expressing eloquent enthusiasm for the USSR and for the cause of the Spanish revolution.[19]

The quest for unity was complicated by the diversities prevailing between different sections of the republic in Spain. Catalonia, the seat of the most modern industry and the second largest city in Spain, had enjoyed since 1932 a quasi-autonomous status within the republic, its internal affairs being administered by an elected council, the Generalitat, a title which recalled the independence of the province in medieval times. Companys, the president of the Generalitat and leader of the bourgeois Catalan party Esquerra, had proclaimed the independence of Catalonia at the time of the Asturias revolt of October 1934, and had narrowly escaped execution when the revolt was suppressed. Of the Catalan workers' organizations the anarchist CGT was the largest and most powerful, the socialist UGT trailing far behind. The Catalan communists under the leadership of Nin and Maurín had broken away from the PCE in 1930 and 1931,[20] and dissolved into several warring groups of Left communists. In February 1935, these groups reunited to form a Partido Obrero de Unificación Marxista (POUM). The membership of POUM did not exceed a few thousand. But its revolutionary ardour far outstripped that of the PCE, which was now preaching caution and moderation in the name of the popular front, and, moreover, was lukewarm on Catalan demands for greater independence. POUM supported the popular front in the elections of 1936. However, sparring soon began between it and the PCE. *La Batalla*, the organ of POUM, attacked "the fundamentally false position of the working-class parties in supporting the bourgeois

---

[18] J. Díaz, *Tres Años de Lucha* (Paris, 1970), pp. 168–182; *Rundschau*, No. 19, April 23, 1936, pp. 778–779.

[19] *Ibid*. No. 21, May 7, 1936, pp. 851–852, 868–869.

[20] See *The Twilight of Comintern, 1930–1935* (1982), pp. 291–292, 299.

government", and raised the banner of red revolution and Spanish Soviets. The PCE journal retorted by denouncing the "renegade" Maurín as "an enemy of the popular front".[21] The persistent sniping of this dissident and extremely vocal group was a thorn in the side of the PCE, and lent colour to the allegation that it stood nearer to its bourgeois allies in the popular front than to the unimpeachably proletarian POUM.

At a session of the presidium of IKKI on May 22, 1936, Hernández presented a report on the PCE which sounded more clearly the note of caution. The aim of the party was to ensure "the complete victory of democratic and revolutionary forces over Fascism and counter-revolution", and "massive support" for the popular front was to be sought in the workers' and peasants' alliances. The PCE "loyally supports the Left republican government", but without renouncing the right of criticism or of the pursuit of its own independent policy. It stood for trade union unity, and for a *rapprochement* with the anarchist CNT, and eventually for union with the PSOE and the creation of "one revolutionary party of the Spanish proletariat". It decisively rejected "the provocative burning down of churches and monasteries, since such acts only go to help counter-revolution". Dimitrov, intervening in the debate, tilted the balance still further in favour of caution. He praised the PCE for its critical attitude to "the Leftist slogans of the Left socialists headed by Largo Caballero, who propose to begin immediately the struggle for a socialist republic". The present task was to carry the bourgeois democratic revolution to its conclusion. At the end of the session, the secretariat of IKKI registered a resolution declaring "that the fundamental and urgent line of the PCE and the Spanish proletariat" was "to carry out measures aimed at the completion of the democratic revolution". It approved the efforts of the PCE to come to terms with social-democratic and anarcho-syndicalist workers, and to seek methods of approach to the Catholic masses. It added that the question of the participation of communists in a popular front government would be "decided in accordance with the interests of the popular front in the struggle against Fascism and counter-revolution".[22] The question which had been decided

---

[21] *La Batalla*, April 10, 1936; *Mundo Obrero*, April 24, 1936 (cited in S. Payne, *The Spanish Revolution* [1970], p. 199).
[22] Hernández's report is summarized in *Kommunisticheskii Internatsional* No. 11–12, (1936), pp. 131–132. For Dimitrov's intervention see *Georgii*

in the negative for the PCF was left open for the PCE. These hesitations no doubt reflected divided counsels in the Comintern hierarchy. A congress of the PCE was projected for the summer of 1936, but, owing to the outbreak of the civil war, never took place.[23]

The mood of euphoria induced in the Spanish Left by the electoral victory of the popular front, and faith in the rising tide of revolution, were profoundly illusory. A minor re-shuffle of governmental posts took place. Azaña, the leader of the so-called "Republican Left", had formed a government after the elections. In May he replaced Alcalá Zamora as president of the republic, and was succeeded as Prime Minister by one of his followers, the colourless Casares Quiroga, the Left wing of the PSOE having vetoed the appointment of Prieto. In essence, nothing had changed. Neither the Cortes nor the government had the authority or the cohesion to carry out, or even to formulate, a programme of social reform. Unity did not extend beyond a vague belief in the virtues of a democratic republic. A minor achievement of the regime was the establishment of regular diplomatic relations with the USSR. The initial approach was made at Geneva in April 1936 by Madariaga, the Spanish delegate at the League of Nations, and was welcomed by Litvinov; but it was not until August 31, after the outbreak of civil war, that Rozenberg, the first Soviet Ambassador to Spain, presented his credentials in Madrid.[24]

The government rested on hollow foundations, which revealed the essential weakness of Spanish democracy. A fragmented Left confronted a determined and increasingly desperate Right. If the election had been a victory for the Left, it had not been a defeat for the Right, which had actually increased its vote at the expense of the Centre. In spite of gestures of a desire for unity between leaders, the loyalty of the workers was divided between the socialist and anarchist trade union federations (UGT and CNT); fisticuffs, and sometimes shooting, marked bitter mutual

Dimitrov: *Vydayushchiisya Deyatel' Kommunisticheskogo Dvizheniya* (1972), pp. 335–338, which also mentions conversations between Dimitrov and Codovilla, oddly described as "one of the leaders of the PCE"; for the resolution see *Kommunisticheskii Internatsional: Kratkii Istoricheskii Ocherk* (1969), pp. 438–439.

[23] *Georgii Dimitrov: Vydayushchiisya Deyatel' Kommunisticheskogo Dvizheniya* (1972), p. 336, note 2.

[24] *Dokumenty Vneshnei Politiki SSSR*, xix (1974), 230, 416–417.

animosities between their members. Largo Caballero toured the country making revolutionary speeches, though the applause of the PCE for his efforts was tempered by jealousy of his ambition to appear as the charismatic leader of the revolution, and by the restraint imposed by Codovilla, in the name of Comintern, on exhibitions of revolutionary ardour. Largo Caballero's fiery eloquence frightened the moderates in the PSOE, as well as the bourgeois radical supporters of the popular front, and provided the Right with the provocation it needed. The role of the PCE scarcely counted. For a few weeks the army and the politicians of the Right, CEDA and the Falange, hesitated to move; the prospect of establishing an authoritarian regime by constitutional means still restrained them from more extreme measures. But, as the sultry Spanish summer set in, it was clear that these inhibitions would not last, and that the storm was about to break.

❒2❒
THE ATTACK

It began on July 17–18, 1936, when the army garrisons in Spanish Morocco proclaimed a revolt against the republican government. Their example was quickly followed in most garrison towns of southern and western Spain. The suddenness of the outbreak, the rapidity with which it spread from one place to another, and the ease with which resistance to it was overwhelmed, suggested a movement which had been expected and desired and planned by a large number of people for some time. On July 19, General Franco arrived in Morocco from the Canary Islands, where he had been posted by the government to keep him out of the way, placed himself at the head of the rebellion, and announced his intention to constitute an alternative Spanish government. On the same day the government in Madrid resigned; and Casares Quiroga was succeeded as Prime Minister by another republican standing slightly further to the Left, Giral. On the first news of the uprising, on July 18, 1936, the PCE newspaper *Mundo Obrero* published a call to "workers" and "anti-Fascists" to rally to the defence of the republic against "criminal attacks".[1] And this was followed by an appeal over the Madrid radio by Dolores Ibárruri, addressed to "Workers, Anti-Fascists, Working People", as well as to "the peoples of Catalonia, the Basque region, Galicia and all Spaniards", to rise in defence of "popular liberty and the democratic achievements of the people".[2] The dominant personality and impassioned eloquence of this remarkable woman, known everywhere as "La Pasionaria", remained throughout the civil war an asset of the republican, and specifically the communist, cause.

The battle-lines between rebel-held, or "nationalist", territory and "republican" territory held by the government were quickly drawn. The last desperate act of the outgoing government had been the distribution of arms from army depots and barracks to

---

[1] Quoted in *Rundschau*, No. 33, July 23, 1936, pp. 1326–1327.
[2] *Mundo Obrero*, July 20, 1936.

workers' militias. These unique military detachments, recruited by the trades unions and Left political parties on a voluntary basis, made up in revolutionary enthusiasm for what they lacked in military training and discipline.[3] During August 1936 the government continued to appeal for the recruitment of a "volunteer army" to defend the republic. On September 14 the PCE militias, which came to be known as the "Fifth Regiment", called for a levy of 10,000 volunteers.[4] Thanks to the militias, supported by loyal units of the regular army and the civil guard, risings in Madrid and in the industrial cities of the north were nipped in the bud, though not without some heavy street fighting in Barcelona.

In the first weeks of the rising, the nationalists established control of the whole of western Spain up to the French frontier at Irún, the mining and industrial region of Asturias in the north remaining a republican enclave in nationalist territory. Eastern Spain, from Catalonia with its capital Barcelona in the north, to Málaga in the south, was loyal to the republic. The area around Madrid formed a broad promontory projecting into nationalist territory, which threatened it from three sides. A shifting frontier was manned, not very effectively, by both armies. Gains and losses were registered. But direct engagements were comparatively few. The main industrial regions, with the two largest cities, remained in republican hands; and that division was significant of the social rift which lay at the root of the conflict. The traditional ruling classes of Spain, long apprehensive of the slide in Spanish politics towards the Left, combined with the upper strata of the rising bourgeoisie to form a new Right, which looked to Franco as its saviour. The democratic republicans and the workers were determined to resist any attempt to whittle away the gains which they had won, and those which they still hoped to win, from a democratically elected government. The cause of the Left was weakened both by the lack of cohesion between workers and bourgeois republicans and by the deep split in the ranks of the workers between socialists and anarchists. But the challenge

[3] For a description of them, see *Collected Essays, Journalism and Letters of George Orwell*, i (1968), pp. 316–328; officers and men received equal pay, and mingled "on terms of complete equality" (*ibid*. i, p. 272).

[4] *Pod Znamenem Ispanskoi Respubliki* (1975), p. 378, note 3; *Mundo Obrero*, September 14, 1936. For the communist "Fifth Regiment" see p. 22 below.

from Franco imparted to the popular front a revolutionary fervour which it had hitherto lacked, and which still further alarmed the nationalist Right. These divisions accounted for the extreme bitterness and savagery with which the war was conducted from the outset. In nationalist territory, workers and peasants who resisted or wavered were intimidated by military tribunals and mass executions. In government territory, the Catholic church, always a bulwark of reaction in Spanish politics, became a popular target of attack. The burning of churches was an everyday occurrence, and the killing of priests not rare. These atrocities were a regular feature of the propaganda of the Right, especially in foreign countries.

The Spanish civil war became an international issue. Franco's Manifesto of Las Palmas, broadcast at dawn on July 18, 1936, may not have attracted much attention in Paris or in London, but it must have been heard with satisfaction in Berlin and Rome.[5] Franco called on all those who felt a "sacred love for Spain" to rescue her from anarchy fomented by "government-appointed authorities" and "revolutionary hordes obeying orders...from foreign elements". He pointed his finger directly at "Soviet agents" who exploited the "unheeding spirit of the masses". A few days later he appealed urgently to Mussolini and then to Hitler for military aid, especially for aeroplanes and flying officers, since the weak Spanish air force, unlike the army, had remained solidly on the side of the government. Mussolini, already intoxicated by his success in Abyssinia, eagerly seized on the opportunity to advance his project of making the Mediterranean an Italian sea. Hitler, though less directly concerned, enjoyed the prospect of weakening and embarrassing France, and creating a Fascist state in western Europe. Both complied with Franco's request. Within a few days aeroplanes, military supplies and technical personnel were reaching Spain in significant numbers; at a later stage, units of the Italian army, in the guise of volunteers, appeared on the scene. But the Italian aid always exceeded the German, in quantity if not in quality. No German ground forces were engaged in Spain.

While Franco looked for help from Rome and Berlin, Giral turned to Paris. A telephone call to Blum on July 20, 1936, asking

---

[5] The text of the Manifesto of Las Palmas is given in Brian Crozier, *Franco: A Biographical History* (London, 1967), Appendix 4, pp. 519–22.

for help in obtaining arms and aeroplanes from France, elicited a sympathetic reply;[6] and the PCE appealed desperately to the PCF.[7] Left-wing opinion in the western countries had been immediately vociferous in support of the republic. On July 21, 1936, the Committee against War and Fascism in Paris sent telegrams of sympathy to Azaña and Giral, and issued an appeal for help to "all friends of freedom and peace".[8] Two days later, the leaders of the Second International and Amsterdam International, in joint session in Brussels, called on all democratic countries to aid the Spanish workers and peasants in their struggle for democracy and for the republic.[9]

The response of the Western communist parties showed an eagerness to fit the campaign for the defence of the Spanish republic into the framework of the popular front. Thorez, in a speech of July 25, 1936, at Amiens on the tasks and achievements of the popular front, added that "our thoughts and our hearts are with the Spanish republicans and their government, with those who are facing with courage the assault of the Fascists"; and a week later in Paris he insisted that the Spanish government was a legal government based on a parliamentary majority and on respect for property, that it was "a calumny to allege that the struggle is for communism, for the dictatorship of the proletariat", and that the issue was the defence of the republican constitution.[10] In Britain Pollitt spoke in the same vein. The struggle had been "forced on the Spanish people in the attempt to restore feudal, monarchist and clerical reactionaries to power"; the Spanish people were "not fighting to establish Soviets or the proletarian dictatorship", but to maintain democracy. Internationally, Spain had been selected by the Fascist aggressors "to strike the first blow in a new Fascist offensive". Pollitt ended by calling on the British National Government to come to the aid of "the elected people's government" of Spain, by demanding "the immediate mobilization of the forces and powers at the disposal of the League of Nations", and by proposing a joint appeal to the

---

[6] G. Lefranc, *Le Front Populaire* (1974), p. 185.
[7] J. Duclos, *Mémoires*, ii (1969), p. 168, records several telephone conversations with Uribe, a leading member of the PCE and future communist minister in the Spanish government.
[8] *Rundschau*, No. 33, July 23, 1936, pp. 1328–1329.
[9] *Ibid*. No. 34, July 30, 1936, p. 1376.
[10] *Oeuvres de Maurice Thorez*, III, xii (1954), 133, 147–149.

National Government with the Labour Party, the TUC and the Cooperative Party to "compel it to support the Spanish Government".[11]

The initial response of the French popular front government to Giral's request was moulded by this powerful sentiment of sympathy for the republic; and in the first days of the civil war aeroplanes and other arms and munitions were despatched to Spain. But French opinion was seriously divided. Influential conservative and Catholic circles actively supported Franco. The bogey of communism could still be invoked with effect.[12] Pacifism and fear of involvement in war were strong in the Left. British opinion, like French opinion, was divided, though sympathy for the republican government was not confined to the Left. The armaments industry in Britain was not nationalized; and this absolved the British government from any formal decision. It did not interfere with shipments of arms and munitions to Spain, while doing nothing to promote them. The predominantly conservative British government stood, however, well to the Right of the French popular front; and, when Blum visited London on July 23, Eden is said to have warned him of the dangers of involvement in the supply of arms to the republicans, and indicated that the British government intended to remain neutral in the Spanish war.[13]

When Blum returned to Paris, he found that Right-wing hostility to support for the Spanish Left had intensified, and that even among his own ministers opinion had hardened against involvement in the Spanish conflict. At a meeting of the council of ministers on July 25, Delbos and Daladier came out against aid to Spain, while Cot spoke resolutely in favour of it. Blum hedged. He would have liked to continue the supply of arms and planes, but only if it could be done in secret, or in the guise of aid from Mexico, the only country which had ranged itself openly on the

[11] *Daily Worker*, August 6, 1936.

[12] *The Times* correspondent in Paris, who doubtless had contacts on the Right, reported that "the prospect of a communist reign of terror in Spain is scarcely, if at all, more agreeable than that of a Fascist or a military dictatorship" (*The Times*, August 1, 1936).

[13] Eden in his memoirs disclaimed any recollection of a discussion of Spanish affairs on this occasion (for the conflicting evidence see H. Thomas, *The Spanish Civil War* [3rd edn, 1977], p. 344); but the subsequent action of both governments supports the assumption that an exchange of views did take place.

side of the republican Spanish government. In the end, a farcical situation seems to have arisen in which Delbos, the Minister for Foreign Affairs, sought to prevent an export of aeroplanes to Spain organized by Cot, the Minister for Air.

Reactions in the USSR were as hesitant as those in France and Great Britain. Public expressions of sympathy for the Spanish government and denunciation of the rebels were combined with official reticence. Determination to keep the foreign policy of the USSR in line with that of France and Britain, its political allies against the menace of the Fascist powers, was a dominant force in Moscow at this time. Influential circles in the Russian party, like most Leftists in the Western countries, pressed for support for the Spanish republic. But this pressure was, for the time being, subjected to the restraint of diplomatic expediency. That this restraint quickly broke down, in the USSR though not in the West, was due not so much to the weight of sympathy and support for the Spanish revolution, as to fear, not apparently shared in the Western democracies, of the danger of submitting passively to constant bouts of Fascist aggression. Not to resist the victory of German and Italian ambitions in Spain seemed both cowardly and, in the long term, dangerous.

No word came from the Soviet government or from Comintern. Opinion in both institutions on so awkward a question was likely to be divided. The French military attaché in Moscow, relying doubtless on intelligence sources, reported to Paris on August 13, 1936, that two factions existed in Comintern: a "moderate faction", to which Stalin belonged, and which "desired to avoid any intervention in order not to provoke a reaction from Germany and Italy", and an "extremist faction" which "considers that the USSR cannot remain neutral and must support the legal government". It is most unlikely that Stalin concerned himself with debates in Comintern. But at this time he evidently shared Litvinov's anxiety to do nothing that might antagonize the French government. The report added that the extremists were liable to be accused of "Trotskyism", and that their intransigent attitude might "lead to measures of repression, extending for the Russians even to deportation".[14] The impending indictment and trial of Zinoviev and his co-defendants had not yet been announced. But rumours of something afoot were evidently already circulating in

[14] *Documents Diplomatiques Français, 1932–1939*, 2me Série, iii (1966), 208.

Moscow. The Spanish crisis could hardly have failed to increase the tension, though it was not mentioned in the proceedings of the Zinoviev-Kamenev trial.

Articles in the press treated Franco as a tool of aggressive Italian and German Fascists. A leading article in *Pravda* on August 1, 1936, on the theme "Fascism Means War", accused Germany of having provoked the rebellion in Spain, of helping it with arms and money, and of bombarding Spanish ports. But the only decision taken was to give financial aid to the republicans through the trades unions.[15] Collections were at once set afoot in the trades unions, and the columns of *Pravda* in the first days of August were full of accounts of the generous response. On August 3 a mass demonstration was held in the Red Square in Moscow, at which 120,000 workers listened to an eloquent appeal by Shvernik for aid for the Spanish republic, and shouted "Down with Franco".[16] Two days later it was announced that a total of more than 12 million rubles had been raised, and that Shvernik had despatched the equivalent in francs to Giral for the use of the Spanish government.[17] No mention was made of the sending of arms – or, indeed, of any other form of aid – from the USSR to Spain at this time.

Meanwhile, the French government, anxious to extricate itself from its embarrassing situation, conceived the project of securing from the governments concerned a mutual undertaking to refrain from intervention in the Spanish conflict and from the supply of war material to either party. The idea was initially communicated to Britain and Italy on August 1, 1936. The British government enthusiastically approved, and suggested that a similar approach should be made to Portugal, Germany and the USSR. This was done. On August 5 the Soviet government announced its

[15] According to a report from Spanish nationalist sources, the decision was taken at a joint meeting of the executive committee of Comintern and Profintern in Moscow presided over by Monmousseau on July 21, 1936 (H. Thomas, *The Spanish Civil War* [3rd edn, 1977], pp. 338, note 4, 360); this report, which appears to emanate from the none too reliable Vassart (see *The Twilight of Comintern, 1930–1935* [1982], p. 194, note 128), must be treated with caution.

[16] *Pravda*, August 4, 1936; M. Kol'tsov, *Ispanskii Dnevnik* (2nd edn, 1958), pp. 11–12; among those present were Fadeev, the president of the Council of Soviet Writers, and Fersman, a member of the presidium of the Academy of Sciences (*Pod Znamenem Ispanskoi Respubliki* [1965], p. 59).

[17] M. Kol'tsov, *Ispanskii Dnevnik* (2nd edn, 1958), p. 113; *Pravda*, August 6, 1936.

acceptance in principle of the proposal; and the other governments, after some hesitation, took the same course. The text of a declaration on non-intervention was drafted by the French government, endorsed by the British government on August 15, and submitted to the other prospective signatories. Soviet acceptance took the form of an exchange of notes with the French Ambassador in Moscow on August 23. The Soviet government made the proviso that it would put the declaration in force as soon as Germany, Italy and Portugal had formally acceded to it. This was achieved on the following day. Twenty-one other European countries, some of them not even remotely concerned, acceded later. The French government, by way of demonstrating its good faith, placed an embargo on August 8 on exports of arms and munitions to Spain. The British government followed suit on August 15, the Soviet government on August 28.[18]

The non-intervention declaration was tainted with hypocrisy from the outset. Nobody believed that it would be observed; and two, at least, of the signatories had no intention of observing it. Soviet acceptance, in view of the campaign, in the USSR and in communist parties abroad, in support of the republican government, seemed at first sight a surprising gesture. But the USSR lacked the capacity to send military supplies to Spain on any scale matching that of Germany and Italy. It can hardly have been supposed in Moscow that Germany or Italy would be induced by a diplomatic agreement to suspend the supply of arms to Franco. But, if they violated the agreement, it would be all the easier to discredit them in the eyes of the Western world; and any shipments which might be made from the USSR would be condoned as a measure of retaliation. The main underlying motive, however, was undoubtedly the desire to keep in step with the two Western powers. To reject a proposal made by France, and strongly backed by Britain, would have placed the Soviet government in a position of isolation which it most of all dreaded. Soviet accession to the agreement was explained by Litvinov a month later in his speech to the League of Nations Assembly in Geneva. The Soviet government had not wished to offend "a friendly country" which was afraid, in the opposite event, of "an inter-

---

[18] The best short account of these proceedings is in A. J. Toynbee, *Survey of International Affairs, 1937*, ii (1938), 223, 232–244; for the text of the Franco–Soviet exchange of notes see *Dokumenty Vneshnei Politiki SSSR*, xix (1974), 402–403.

national conflict". Nevertheless, it "considers the principle of neutrality inapplicable to a struggle of rebels against a legal government, and contrary to the rules of international law".[19] On the proposal of the British government, a committee was set up to supervise the execution of the agreement. It met for the first time in London in September, and dragged on for many months in an atmosphere of frustration and unreality.

[19] *Ibid*. xix, 446.

⬜3⬜
THE NON-INTERVENTION COMMITTEE

The successes of the nationalist forces, now within striking, or bombing, distance of Madrid, did nothing to enhance the prestige or the confidence of the republican government. On September 4, 1936, Giral resigned, and was succeeded as Prime Minister and Minister for War by Largo Caballero, whose undiminished vigour and effervescent oratory had helped to preserve his popularity. The new government marked a swing to the Left, but was broadly based. Of six members of the PSOE, two belonged to its Right wing: Largo Caballero's old rival and enemy Prieto,[1] as Minister of Navy and for Air, and Negrín, as Minister for Finance. Both anarchists and communists were invited to join. The anarchists refused. The PCE, availing itself of the choice left open by the decision of the IKKI secretariat of May 22,[2] decided to accept, and two communist ministers entered the government. It was the first example of communist participation in a non-communist government.

The nationalist rebellion presented no problems either of ideology or of tactics to the PCE. The broadest possible anti-Fascist front was the need of the moment. The party newspaper *Mundo Obrero* of July 18, 1936, appealed to "workers", "anti-Fascists", to all working people, and ended its call with the slogan "Long Live the Democratic Republic".[3] In a crisis of this kind one did not look further ahead. Hernández, one of the new communist ministers, had already written in a party journal denying that "the present workers' movement has for its objective the establishment of a proletarian dictatorship after the revolution is ended".[4] Antonio Mije, a member of the PCE politburo, defended the decision to join the government at a

---

[1] Prieto did not conceal his low opinion of Largo Caballero (M. Kol'tsov, *Ispanskii Dnevnik* [2nd edn, 1958], pp. 73–74, 85).

[2] See p. 7 above.

[3] Quoted in *Rundschau*, No. 33, July 23, 1936, pp. 1326–1327.

[4] *Mundo Obrero*, August 9, 1936.

party meeting on September 8, which was also attended by Marty and Duclos, with a number of arguments, beginning with the need to close ranks against reaction and Fascism, and ending with the claim that "in immediate connection with the war the chief tasks of the democratic bourgeois revolution are being fulfilled".[5] When the Cortes met on October 1, it gave to the new ministers a vote of confidence. Díaz pointedly remarked that the government was "a continuation of its predecessor", and "a government under whose leadership we shall fight and conquer all the enemies of the republic and of Spain".[6]

In the corridors of Comintern in Moscow, far removed from the scene of action, the issues seemed less clear. It was not until September 18, 1936, that the secretariat of IKKI, reassembled after the summer vacation, set out to define the attitude of Comintern to the Spanish war, now just two months old. Nobody quite knew what to do or say; and the shock of the trials and executions of Zinoviev and Kamenev made officials unusually reluctant to venture on what might be treacherous ground. The unnamed Spanish delegate admitted in his report that "intensive aid to the rebels from Germany, Italy and Portugal" had prevented the government from crushing the rebellion and had prolonged the civil war. But he presented a highly pragmatic programme of action for the PCE. The party claimed to have persuaded other parties to agree to the formation of a regular people's army under a unified command. It stood for iron discipline at the front, the organization of the rear, and the organization of production in the factories for military means. While it looked forward to "a revolutionary re-shaping of agrarian relations", it must take suitable measures for the collection of the harvest and for the extension of cultivation. The motto must be: "All for the popular front, all through the popular front."[7] After Manuilsky had posed the familiar dilemma of the character, bourgeois-democratic or proletarian, of the Spanish revolution, Dimitrov boldly cut the Gordian knot by rejecting "the old canons of social-democracy which existed 20 or 30 years ago". The state for which the Spanish people were fighting would be not an old-style democratic republic, but "a special state with genuine

[5] *Rundschau*, No. 42, September 17, 1936, pp. 1745–1746.
[6] M. Kol'tsov, *Ispanskii Dnevnik* (2nd edn, 1958), p. 149.
[7] *Kommunisticheskii Internatsional*, No. 15 (1936), p. 114.

people's democracy". It would be "not a Soviet state but an anti-Fascist state, with the participation of the genuinely Left part of the bourgeoisie". Reviving Lenin's formula of 1905, he called it "a special form of democratic dictatorship of the working class and the peasantry". Collectivization of land and of industrial enterprises could wait. What was at stake was "victory over Fascism". With the same end in view, Dimitrov insisted on the merging of the workers' militia, now well-armed and organized units, with the loyal elements in the regular army, in a single "republican army" – a burning issue ever since the entry of the PCE into the government. Speeches by Kuusinen, Codovilla, Pieck, Gottwald, Pollitt and others are not on record.[8]

At this meeting, Dimitrov's oratory seems to have carried all before it. But his cavalier treatment of cherished party doctrine cannot have pleased the hard-line defenders of orthodoxy. The irrepressible Knorin, in an article in *Pravda* which is said to have incurred the wrath of Manuilsky, cast doubt on the possibility of transforming the current bourgeois revolution in Spain into a socialist revolution; the bourgeoisie was too much tied up with tradition, the church and counter-revolution. The popular front in Spain was too weak to achieve revolutionary aims.[9] Togliatti's fluent pen was enlisted to allay the controversy. In an article "On the Peculiarity of the Spanish Revolution", which had wide publicity, he described it as "the greatest event since October 1917 in the history of struggle for liberation". It had the character of "a national-revolutionary war", since defeat would mean the enslavement of Spain to German and Italian Fascism; it was also a struggle for freedom for Basques and Catalans. The immediate task was to achieve a bourgeois-democratic revolution in the poorest and most backward of European countries. The working class had struck the first blow against Fascism in October 1934 in Asturias. But a real communist party in Spain existed only since 1931. The PCE was weak, and the PSOE was stronger than the Mensheviks had ever been; and anarcho-syndicalist mass organ-

---

[8] Accounts of the session in *Kommunisticheskii Internatsional: Kratkii Istoricheskii Ocherk* (1969), pp. 439–440, and *Georgii Dimitrov: Vydayushchiisya Deyatel' Kommunisticheskogo Dvizheniya* (1972), pp. 253–254, 339–340, are limited almost exclusively to Dimitrov's speech, an extract from which appeared in *Voprosy Istorii KPSS*, No. 3 (1969), pp. 12–13.

[9] *Pravda*, October 3, 1936; *Georgii Dimitrov: Vydayushchiisya Revolutsioner-Leninets* (1972), p. 153.

izations were an obstacle to the action of a true, disciplined proletariat. So were premature demands for a "collectivization" of
land and factories, abolition of money, etc. It had to be
recognized that part of the bourgeoisie and petty bourgeoisie were
political allies in resisting Fascism. A plethora of arguments
pointed implicitly to the need for caution and moderation. The
whole article was attuned to Dimitrov's pragmatism rather than
to the ideological purity of Knorin.[10]

The civil war made Spain, for the first time for many years, a
centre of prime interest and concern in the capitals of Europe,
not least Moscow. On August 8, 1936, a leading Soviet journalist,
Kol'tsov, arrived in Madrid as a correspondent of *Pravda*, and
was followed by the well-known writer Ehrenburg as a correspondent of *Izvestiya*.[11] On August 27, the first Soviet ambassador to
Spain, Rozenberg, a former deputy secretary-general of the
League of Nations, arrived in Madrid, with an impressive retinue
of military, naval and air attachés and experts. The appointment
of Antonov-Ovseenko as Soviet consul-general in Barcelona was
also significant; he had won distinction as a military commander
in the 1917 revolution and the ensuing civil war. The supply of
military equipment from the USSR was to come later. But from
this moment the armies of the republic did not lack the support
and encouragement of Soviet military advisers. The first problem
was to integrate those units of the regular army which had
remained loyal to the republic with the workers' militias created
by trades unions and parties of the Left, which constituted the
major part of the republican forces. The communist militia,
more officially designated the Fifth Regiment,[12] appointed a
political commissar on the model of units of the Red Army. Other
militias were persuaded to follow that example. An organization
of political commissars was set up with Álvarez del Vayo, the
Foreign Minister, as commissar-general; and this proved an
effective means both of unifying the armed forces and of bringing
them under communist control.

Still more important was the recruitment of International
Brigades. Ever since the outbreak of the civil war, substantial

[10] P. Togliatti, *Opere*, IV, i (1979), 139–154.
[11] M. Kol'tsov, *Ispanskii Dnevnik* (2nd edn, 1958), p. 13.
[12] For an enthusiastic account of the Fifth Regiment see M. Kol'tsov,
Ispanskii Dnevnik (2nd edn, 1958), pp. 115–118.

numbers of foreign volunteers, moved by sympathy for the republican cause, had come to Spain to help in resistance to Franco. The French contingent was initially the most numerous. But the French were soon joined by many other nationalities, including Germans and Italians living in exile. As their number increased, they were organized in brigades, predominantly, though not rigidly, on national lines. European communist parties were instructed by Comintern to conduct recruiting campaigns for the brigades, though by no means all so recruited were communists, and many volunteers went independently.[13] No Russian joined the international brigades. But the commander of the First Brigade was a leading Comintern military expert who had recently worked in China. Born in Austria–Hungary, and taken prisoner by the Russians in the First World War, his real name was Stern; he appeared in Spain under the title of General Kléber.[14]

The most crucial issue was, however, the supply of military equipment, especially tanks and aeroplanes, to the Spanish government. The hollowness of the non-intervention agreement was quickly shown up. The meetings of the non-intervention committee soon degenerated into farce, being occupied with procedural wrangles, mutual recriminations, and denials of notorious facts. Throughout September 1936, while the flow of arms and equipment to the nationalists from Italy and Germany steadily increased, the ban on shipments from France, Britain and the USSR to republican Spain remained effective. The nationalist forces pressed forward. At the end of September Toledo fell, after some particularly bloody fighting, and Madrid was threatened from the south and west. Frantic appeals to the Spanish people from the government and from the PCE for unity to resist the Fascist onslaught referred to "the substantial help from abroad" received by the army, but refrained from any reproach at the failure of its friends to come to the aid of the republic.[15] A demonstration in Moscow in support of the Spanish

---

[13] The "official" story of recruitment for the British battalion by the CPGB is told in W. Rust, *Britons in Spain* (1939); George Orwell, who recounts his experiences in *Homage to Catalonia* (1938), was sponsored by the ILP.

[14] For his service in China see *The Twilight of Comintern, 1930–1935* (1982), p. 360.

[15] *Rundschau*, No. 44, October 1, 1936, p. 1843.

democratic republic was attended by 100,000 people and addressed by Nikolaeva, who pleaded for "the most extensive help for the fighters, women and children of Spain".[16] But all public statements at this time about shipments from the USSR to Spain emphasized that they consisted of food and other supplies for the civilian population. Many people in Spain and elsewhere must have had a sense of the betrayal of the republican cause by the USSR and by the popular front in the Western democracies.

At what precise moment, and in what circumstances, the decision was taken in Moscow to supply arms to Spain, remains uncertain. Soviet sources stoutly maintained that ships loaded in Odessa for Spanish ports – the *Neva*, which reached Alicante on September 26, 1936, to be followed a few days later by the *Kuban* – carried only non-military supplies for the Spanish people.[17] German and Italian agents purported to know that they contained military machines and material.[18] Krivitsky, at this time working for Soviet Intelligence in Europe, subsequently related that the first communication from Moscow about Spain reached him on September 2, when he was instructed to organize the purchase of arms for the Spanish government in European countries, and their shipment to Spain. This throws no light on the question of the supply of arms from the USSR.[19] According to the same dubious source, Yagoda and two other high officials of the NKVD,

---

[16] *Ibid.* No. 44, October 1, 1936, p. 1848; for Nikolaeva, see *Foundations of a Planned Economy*, Vol. 1, p. 685.

[17] *Pod Znamenem Ispanskoi Respubliki* (1965), p. 60.

[18] Recriminations on these lines occurred in the non-intervention committee about the *Kuban* which sailed from Odessa for Spain on September 27 (*Rundschau*, No. 44, October 1, 1936, pp. 1848–1849; D. Cattell, *Soviet Diplomacy and the Spanish Civil War* [1957], p. 54, quoting unpublished records of the non-intervention committee); an independent witness of the unloading of the *Kuban* in Alicante confirms the Soviet version (J. Martín Blázquez, *I Helped to Build an Army* [1939], pp. 248, 250–251). According to M. Meshcheryakov, *Ispanskaya Respublika i Komintern* (1981), p. 52, the first consignment of Soviet arms arrived in Cartagena on a Spanish ship on October 4; 50 tanks arrived in Cartagena on October 14 on a Soviet ship.

[19] W. Krivitsky, *I Was Stalin's Agent* (1939), p. 100. Krivitsky announced his defection, following the purges in Moscow, in Trotsky's *Byulleten' Oppozitsii* (Paris), No. 60–61, December 1937, pp. 8–10, and settled in 1938 in New York. His book, which first appeared in the form of articles in the *Saturday Evening Post*, was evidently ghosted by an American journalist, and it is difficult to extract the nuggets of information which it undoubtedly contains from the sensational dross in which they are embedded. The conclusion in H. Thomas, *The*

together with the head of military intelligence, met in Moscow on September 14 to organize in the greatest secrecy the sending of arms to Spain. Orlov, an NKVD official already in Spain, was to take charge of operations on the spot. The decision, which doubtless had Stalin's formal or tacit approval, was not divulged to Narkomindel or other Soviet departments, or to the Comintern.[20]

It was not until the following month that a public pronouncement was made, and then in ambiguous terms. On October 7, at a particularly heated meeting of the non-intervention committee, the Soviet delegate read a declaration that the Soviet government "cannot agree to turn the non-intervention argument into a screen to cover military aid to the insurgents from some participants in the agreement", and that, "unless violations of the non-intervention agreement are stopped at once, it will consider itself free from the obligations flowing from the agreement".[21]

All inhibitions on the public profession of aid to the Spanish government were now removed. Greetings were exchanged between Largo Caballero and Kalinin;[22] and on October 15, 1936, Stalin sent a brief, but unusually expressive personal telegram to Díaz, as secretary of the central committee of the PCE:

> The toilers of the Soviet Union only fulfil their duty when they give aid to the Spanish revolutionary masses. They are aware that the liberation of Spain from the persecution of Fascist reactionaries is not a private cause of Spaniards, but a universal cause of the whole of advanced and progressive mankind. Fraternal greetings.[23]

Spanish Civil War (1961) p. 263, note 1, that "Krivitsky's evidence must be regarded as tainted unless corroborated" is the voice of prudence; in the third edition of this work (1977), which has been substantially added to and rewritten, the author more readily accepts sensational information from questionable sources.

[20] Krivitsky, *I Was Stalin's Agent* (1939), pp. 100–103; the statement (*ibid.* p. 98) that the decision had been taken at an extraordinary session of the Politburo summoned by Stalin at the end of August is highly implausible.

[21] *Dokumenty Vneshnei Politiki SSSR*, xix (1974), 464; at the next meeting on October 23, the Soviet representative (on this occasion, Maisky) repeated that the Soviet government could not consider itself bound by the agreement "to a greater degree than any of the other participants".

[22] *Ibid.* xix, 477.

[23] Stalin, *Sochineniya*, xiv (Stanford, 1967), 135; this was apparently a reply to

The secretariat of IKKI followed this up on October 19 with a resolution describing the defeat of the Fascist insurgents as "the central and fundamental task" of the PCE and condemning the "mania" of far-fetched projects, tendencies to "create a new society", which threatened to disrupt the popular front.[24] A substantial part of the annual manifesto of IKKI on the anniversary of the Russian Revolution was devoted this year to the Spanish conflagration.[25] The Spanish civil war, in its European setting, was now a major preoccupation of Comintern.

A curious episode of this period was the transfer to Moscow of the very considerable gold reserve of the Bank of Spain. To avert the risk of its falling into the hands of Franco, it was moved in September 1936 to Cartagena, where it was kept for some time underground in a cave. But this, too, seemed an insecure refuge; and it was felt that the safest course would be to remove it from Spanish soil. Paris or London would not be immune to pressure from Franco, and Moscow was the only alternative. The gold was shipped from Cartagena on October 25, reached Odessa on November 6, and was safely deposited in the vaults in Moscow.[26] The transaction was planned and carried out by Largo Caballero and the Finance Minister, Negrín, without – so far as the wisdom goes – any initiative from Moscow. Nobody suggested that it was in any way a counterpart of Soviet aid to Spain.

The first major crisis of the war followed the launching by Franco, in the last days of October 1936, of a massive attack on Madrid. The prestige of the capital was great; and the German and Italian governments undertook, if it fell, to accord official recognition to Franco as the government of Spain. As the nationalist forces moved steadily nearer, something like panic reigned in republican circles. On November 4, the anarchists reconsidered their policy of abstention, and four members of the CNT joined the government, not without some angry resistance

---

a telegram from Díaz of the same date to the central committee of the Russian party appealing for "fraternal aid" (*Dokumenty Vneshnei Politiki SSSR*, xix [1974], 486). For an effusive reply from Díaz, see J. Díaz, *Tres Años de Lucha* (Paris, 1970), p. 241; M. Kol'tsov, *Ispanskii Dnevnik* (1958), p. 179, describes the public enthusiasm in Madrid on the receipt of Stalin's telegram.

[24] *Georgii Dimitrov: Vydayushchiisya Revolyutsioner-Leninets* (1972), pp. 222–223.

[25] *Rundschau*, No. 49, November 5, 1936, pp. 1985–1987.

[26] H. Thomas, *The Spanish Civil War* (3rd edn, 1977), pp. 448–450.

from the rank and file. The precedent of the Russian civil war was constantly invoked; and crowds flocked to see the Soviet film "Chapaev", celebrating the exploits of a civil war hero, which was showing in Madrid at the time.[27]

But the situation of the government in Madrid was now too exposed to be tenable. Azaña, the president, withdrew to Barcelona. Largo Caballero and the other ministers, unwilling to become involved in the complexities of Catalan politics, prepared to transfer the seat of government to Valencia; and the move was effected on November 6. But this move coincided with a turning point in the military operations. Soviet tanks and aeroplanes had appeared for the first time on the battle-front, and proved decisively superior to the German and Italian machines on the nationalist side. The attackers now began to falter. On November 6, an international brigade, consisting of German, French and Polish battalions with a mixture of other nationalities, under the command of "General Kléber", marched through Madrid amid the cheers of the population to take up positions, for the first time, at the front. Before the end of the month, the great offensive against Madrid had petered out. The brigade numbered less than 2000 men. But historical legend assigned to it a more conspicuous role than to the Soviet tanks in repelling the assault. The workers of the world had saved the republic.[28] Official Soviet sources were still, at this time, reticent on the subject of Soviet military aid; Kol'tsov in his diary (*Ispanskii Dnevnik*, 1958) recounts the events of these days in detail without mentioning Soviet tanks or aeroplanes. Marty called Madrid "the Verdun of democracy".[29] It was claimed that, in the following year, 35,000 volunteers from 59 countries had joined the international brigades fighting for the defence of the Spanish republic.[30]

The Spanish civil war inflamed international tensions throughout Europe. By increasing the apprehension in Western countries about Hitler's and Mussolini's aggressive designs, it

[27] M. Kol'tsov, *Ispanskii Dnevnik* (1958), pp. 249–250.

[28] For a characteristic eulogy of the brigade and its commander see *Rundschau*, No. 57, December 17, 1936, pp. 2260–2261.

[29] *Rundschau*, No. 57, December 17, 1936, p. 2259.

[30] B. Leibzon and K. Shirinya, *Povorot v Politike Kominterna* (1975), p. 379; for a list of the brigades see H. Thomas, *The Spanish Civil War* (3rd edn, 1977), pp. 968–969.

created a wave of sympathy, especially in Left circles, not only for the Spanish government, but also for the USSR, which shared their apprehensions to the full; and this sense of common concern muffled the horror and bewilderment provoked by the Soviet purge trials. In Moscow the same motives led to a more benign attitude to France and Britain. The Soviet representative began to co-operate readily in the discussions of the non-intervention committee, agreeing to a scheme for the appointment of observers to supervise the execution of the agreement, and initiating a proposal to extend it by a prohibition on the dispatch of foreign "volunteers" to Spain. When in December 1936 the Spanish government, to the annoyance of the British and French governments, insisted on formally appealing to the Council of the League of Nations under article 11 of the Council against "the armed intervention of Germany and Italy in the Spanish civil war", Litvinov did not attend the session. The USSR, like Britain and France, was represented by a diplomat of second rank, thus depriving the session of any major political significance; and an anodyne resolution was adopted which referred approvingly to the efforts of the non-intervention committee. Soviet diplomacy followed the course set by IKKI of doing nothing liable to antagonize those whose support it needed to repel the Fascist aggressor.

The arrival in Spain of massive Soviet aid, and its dramatic contribution to the defence of Madrid, led to the uncovenanted, and perhaps unforeseen, result of subordinating the policies and contributions of the republic more and more effectively to the influences and directives emanating from Moscow. Strategy and tactics were determined by those who controlled the flow of arms and equipment. Soviet advisers penetrated many institutions of the Spanish government. The PCE, subject to the firm guidance of Comintern, gained enormously in numbers, prestige and authority. Díaz, at the end of 1936, put its numbers at 250,000, of whom 87,000 were industrial workers, 62,000 agricultural workers, and 7000 professional men or intellectuals.[31]

---

[31] J. Díaz, *Tres Años de Lucha* (Paris, 1970), pp. 289–290; for earlier figures of membership see p. 5 above.

The first and most important field of Soviet activity was the reorganization of the army. Ever since the outbreak of the war the PCE had campaigned for the fusion of the surviving units of the old regular army with the workers' militia, to form a unified "people's army".[32] But little was achieved before the arrival of the Soviet advisers and the formation of the international brigades at the end of 1936. The formula of unification was found in the creation, on the analogy of the international brigades, of "mixed brigades" comprising battalions both of the old army and of the militias. The institution of political commissars, introduced into the international brigade, was extended to the mixed brigades, and then to the whole of the new people's army. Since the institution was based on a Soviet model, it was natural that communists should predominate in it. The corps of commissars became a powerful group, whose influence in military affairs was directed to the management of the army and to the establishment of overall Soviet control.[33] The undivided aim of military efficiency was pursued; this, too, coincided with Soviet and Comintern policy at this time. If any ideology was invoked, it was that of patriotism and not of revolution.

The salutary effect of these measures on the fighting power of the republic is beyond question. The whole process was described by a foreign eye-witness not biased in favour of the communists:

> With the siege of Madrid, military leadership, from November 1936 onwards, fell into the hands of the Communists, who launched a totalitarian scheme instead of a revolutionary one. The basic ideas of Communist military policy were: no revolution during the war; strict discipline, including terrorism within the ranks; strict political control of the army, by a system of political "commissars", with the aim of creating an ideology adapted to this policy, an ideology, that is, mainly based on nationalism.[34]

Not everything went smoothly. The anarchists firmly resisted the integration of their numerous and powerful militias. Friction

[32] See p. 20 above.
[33] See p. 22 above.
[34] F. Borkenau, in J. Martín Blásquez, *I Helped to Build an Army* (1939), pp. x–xi.

occurred within the new unified army. Kléber, the commander of the international brigade, hailed as the saviour of Madrid, incurred the jealousy of Miaja, the Spanish commander of the army; he may also have incurred that of his Soviet colleagues. Differences are said to have arisen between him and Miaja: Kléber proposed to go over to the offensive, and Miaja considered this rash and premature. What is clear is that Kléber failed to win the support of his colleagues, or perhaps of the military command in Moscow. He was relieved of his command in January 1937.[35] About the same time, the Communist Fifth Regiment and the international brigades were merged in the people's army.

The security organs of the republic by a similar process quickly came under Soviet control. When the nationalist General Mola announced in October 1936 that he was about to launch the attack on Madrid, with four columns of troops, he added that he also counted on a "fifth column" of supporters in the city itself, thus coining a phrase which passed into international vocabulary. To control this "fifth column", the government relied on a secret police, nominally a department of the Ministry of the Interior, but constituted in separate sections drawn from all the popular front parties, including the anarchists. The communist section was headed by Orlov, the representative of the NKVD in Spain, and this section, by virtue of its larger and more experienced personnel, dominated the activities of the secret police. Spanish politicians had never been subject to the scruples felt in democratic countries about police methods. The methods employed under communist leadership were certainly not benign. But nobody protested, so long as such methods were directed exclusively against members or suspected members of Franco's "fifth column". Later, when the communists turned their weapon against other parties,[36] well-founded denunciations of the communist reign of terror began to be heard.

When the PCE decided to enter the government in September 1936, two not very important ministries, Education and Agriculture, were assigned to it. In the subsequent reorganizations,

[35] The view of this incident in D. Cattell's *Communism and the Spanish Civil War* (1965), pp. 130–131, as a characteristic example of Spanish recalcitrance to Soviet control, and a turning point in Spanish–Soviet military relations, seems highly speculative; had Kléber retained the confidence of Moscow, he could not have been removed.

[36] See pp. 35–36 below.

when communist power had enormously increased, the number of communist ministers was never raised; the party preferred to keep a low profile, and to maintain intact the facade of the popular front. But behind its facade the PCE, as the willing instrument of Soviet authority, continued to advance inexorably towards complete control of the supreme organs of the Spanish government, which became what its enemies called it, the puppet of Moscow. The process was, however, gradual, and was complicated by the situation in Catalonia, where the PCE had to contend with the newly formed POUM. Under the leadership of Nin and Maurín, POUM, although numerically relatively weak, appealed successfully to the more radical sections of the Left.[37]

The PCE, in the face of these dissident groups, had never been able to establish any significant foothold in Catalonia. But, with the outbreak of the civil war, its campaign for the popular front and for unity with the PSOE scored a remarkable success. An agreement was reached between the communists and socialists in Catalonia to set up a joint party, the Partido Socialista Unificado de Catalonia (PSUC). It claimed no more than five or six thousand members. But its importance lay in the control of the Catalan socialist trades unions affiliated to the UGT, said to be 40,000 strong. The new party was at once received into Comintern. Acting with an energy and self-assurance inspired by the prestige and authority of Moscow, the communists soon began to dominate their socialist partners. The PSUC gave the PCE for the first time a solid base in Catalonia.

Another more remarkable success was to come. The anarchists had refused to enter Largo Caballero's government in Madrid at the beginning of September 1936. But as the pressures of the civil war increased, anarchist military formations, though they rejected incorporation into the Spanish people's army, took part in fighting at the front. At the end of September, the CNT agreed to take its place in the Generalitat at Barcelona, together with the PSUC, POUM, and the bourgeois party standing for Catalan independence, the Esquerra. A further stage in the realization of a united front in Catalonia was an agreement signed on October 22 by representatives of the UGT and the CNT. It was a triumph for the communists whose hand guided the UGT negotiators. The social ends of the revolution were

[37] See p. 6 above.

comfortably qualified; and the aims of the parties were declared to include "the ultimate concentration of all forces for final victory", "the introduction of obligatory military service which will mark the beginning of a great people's army" and "the creation of a great war industry".[38] The next step was to extend to Madrid what had been achieved in Barcelona. In November four anarchist ministers joined the central government of Largo Caballero.

The reconstituted government at once faced an awkward decision. Franco's assault on Madrid had brought the city uncomfortably close to the front line, and exposed it to frequent bombing. Azaña, the president of the republic, withdrew to Barcelona. Largo Caballero was unwilling to install himself in an anarchist stronghold; and it was decided to move the seat of government to Valencia. The anarchist ministers were persuaded to agree; and the ministers and their departments, followed by the diplomatic corps, transferred themselves on November 6 from Madrid to Valencia. But the fragility of the coalition was demonstrated in a farcical episode, when anarchist militiamen tried to obstruct this move.[39] Berzin, the chief Soviet military adviser, accompanied the government to Valencia. But the main body of advisers remained in Madrid with Miaja, who was responsible for the defence of the city. Orlov and the representatives of the NKVD also remained behind in Madrid.

At this critical moment, the communist approach to the anarchists met with a warm response in the form of an appeal over Barcelona radio on November 6, 1936, by Durruti, a veteran CNT leader. Addressing himself to "the Catalan people", he spoke of the danger which threatened Madrid, and begged his hearers "to put an end to the intrigues, the in-fighting, and rise to the height of the situation". It was not the moment to think of an increase in wages or a shortening of the working day. Durruti called for "sincerity, especially from the CNT and the FAI"; trade union organizations and political parties must "end dissension once and for all". Discipline at the front must be matched by discipline in the rear. Durruti ended by repeating the slogan said to have been coined by the PCE: "They shall not pass."[40] For

---

[38] D. Cattell, *Communism and the Spanish Civil War* (1965), p. 126.

[39] The fullest account of the move is to be found in J. Álvarez del Vayo, *Freedom's Battle* (1940), pp. 204–208; the writer took part in it.

[40] *Kommunistcheskii Internatsional*, No. 17 (1936), p. 87; for a sketch of

some weeks, the anarchists had the unwonted experience of complimentary references in the PCE and Comintern press. When Durruti was killed at the front a fortnight later, he was eulogized by the PCE in *Pravda* as one of the founders of the popular front;[41] and Antonov-Ovseenko, in an interview in the foreign press, expressed "admiration for the Catalan workers, especially for the anarcho-syndicalists".[42]

These exchanges did not, however, suffice for long to overcome the traditional antipathies between the anarchists and other parties of the Left. The approach of the PCE to the anarchists had been motivated by the desire to anchor the CNT firmly to the popular front, and to secure the whole-hearted participation of the substantial anarchist militias in military operations. But it did not imply any shift in policy, or willingness to compromise with the revolutionary proclivities of the anarchists. On December 15, 1936, the central committee of the PCE issued a long manifesto which, more emphatically than any previous party document, preached the over-riding needs of military defence, and rejected anything which might prejudice military efficiency or antagonize potential allies in the war against the nationalists. It called for reorganization of the armed forces and of the military high command, the enforcement of compulsory military service, and "iron discipline" in the rear. Industry must be geared to the needs of war production, and freed from "the capricious autonomy" of trade unions or groups in single factories. In agriculture that system of tenure, individual or collective, was to be preferred which would ensure maximum production.[43] On December 21, before this document was likely to have reached Moscow, a personal letter was despatched to Largo Caballero bearing the signatures of Stalin, Molotov and Voroshilov, and couched in language rather cruder and more direct than that commonly employed by Comintern. It offered a friendly but emphatic warning not to antagonise the peasants, the petty bourgeoisie and the republicans, who might otherwise "follow the Fascists". Measures of confiscation should be avoided, and freedom of trade

Durruti, see I. Ehrenburg, *Eve of War* (Engl. transl. 1963), pp. 132–135.

[41] *Rundschau*, No. 53, November 27, 1936, p. 2149; for a telegram of condolence from Díaz to Oliver, the leader of the CNT, see *Kommunistcheskii Internatsional*, No. 17 (1936), p. 86.

[42] *Manchester Guardian*, December 22, 1936.

[43] *Rundschau*, No. 1, January 7, 1937, pp. 27–31.

guaranteed. Nothing shall be done to encourage "enemies of Spain" to "regard it as a communist republic". The letter included an enquiry about whether Largo Caballero had found Rozenberg a satisfactory ambassador – a remark which suggested that Rozenberg had fallen out of favour in Moscow.[44] Finally, on December 28, the praesidium of IKKI passed a resolution praising the heroism of the Spanish people, and enthusiastically endorsing the terms of the PCE manifesto of December 15.[45] Codovilla, or some other emissary of IKKI, had probably collaborated in the arrangements of the manifesto. But it would be misleading to treat it as an unqualified product of dictation from Moscow. The influence was reciprocal. The Spanish experience came as a powerful reinforcement to those leaders in Moscow, Dimitrov and others, who were striving to carry the decisions of the seventh congress of Comintern to their logical conclusion, and subordinate the distant prospects of proletarian revolution to the immediate emergency of building a broad basis of resistance to the Fascist danger.

The euphoria bred by the events of the last three months of 1936 – the arrival of Soviet aid, the defeat of Franco's drive against Madrid, the consolidation of the popular front through the entry, first of the PCE, then of the anarchists, into the Madrid government, the growing prestige and influence of the PCE, of the Soviet advisers and of the USSR – was beginning to wear itself out as the new year dawned. It would be difficult to find any one specific moment or cause for the change. Reaction set in against the uncritical enthusiasm and optimism of recent weeks. Irritations multiplied between traditionally hostile parties now suddenly brought together, and between Spaniards and Soviet advisers. As Prime Minister, Largo Caballero had made an important contribution. But the communists had from of old not found him an easy bed-fellow;[46] and his erratic gestures of independence were hard to bear. Most of all, perhaps, the Soviet advisers, and those who directed them from Moscow, intoxicated by their success, suffered from an excess of over-confidence. They became

---

[44] It was first published in the New York Times of June 4, 1939, having been communicated by Araquistáin, who represented the Spanish republic in Paris in 1936–37 and afterwards defected; it was later reprinted in Guerra y Revolución en España, 1936–39, ii (1971), 96–97. See Note A, pp. 86–88 below.

[45] Rundschau, No. 1, January 7, 1937, pp. 31–32.

[46] See p. 2 above.

less wary of offending Spanish susceptibilities; and they showed themselves increasingly prone to embark on policies dictated by either party or Soviet interests rather than by those of the republic.

The first ominous sign was the expulsion of POUM, achieved by the communists with the support of the anarchists in December 1936, from the Generalitat in Barcelona.[47] Nín and Maurín, the founders and leaders of POUM, had long been thorns in the side of the PCE and of Comintern,[48] and did not disguise their total rejection of the authority of Moscow. The communists retaliated by branding them as Trotskyites,[49] a charge not devoid of foundation, though Trotsky himself had repudiated them.[50] It is difficult to dissociate the savage persecution of POUM in Spain, which began at this time, from the purge trials of August 1936 and January 1937 in Moscow, when Zinoviev and Kamenev, Pyatakov and Radek, were arraigned as agents of Trotsky.

Relations between communists and anarchists, who had enjoyed a very brief honeymoon in the last weeks of 1936, also soured in the new year. At the beginning of January 1937, Díaz and a representative of the CNT issued a joint appeal to the members of both organizations deploring "clashes" which had occurred between them.[51] But this gesture was of no avail. Arguments occurred over alleged discrimination in the distribution of arms to POUM militia; and the anarchist FAI, at a conference in February 1937, threatened to withdraw the anarchist militias from the government. It might have been argued that the anarchist and POUM militias were holding the relatively tranquil Aragon front, and that the defenders of Madrid could justly claim priority in the matter of arms. But the complaint was symptomatic of rising mutual anger. The same

---

[47] D. Cattell, *Communism and the Spanish Civil War* (1965), p. 127.

[48] See *The Twilight of Comintern, 1930–1935* (1982), pp. 299, 301, 305.

[49] See, for example, a virulent article by Kol'tsov, entitled "Trotskyist Crimes in Spain", which described POUM as "a Trotskyist organization", and concluded that "wherever the criminal hand of Trotsky reaches, it sows everywhere lies, treason and murder" (*Rundschau*, No. 4, January 29, 1937, p. 146).

[50] For an interview with Trotsky, in which he denied that POUM was Trotskyist, and referred to his numerous articles attacking it, see L. Trotsky, *The Spanish Revolution* (1973), pp. 242–244.

[51] *Rundschau*, No. 1, January 7, 1937, p. 19.

conference unanimously rejected a proposal of the UGT, strongly supported by the communists, for the fusion of the CNT with the UGT.[52] It appears to have been about this time that the security forces, now firmly under communist or Soviet control, began to arrest individual anarchists; and assassinations of prominent anarchists were also reported.

---

[52] For the conference see D. Cattell, *Communism and the Spanish Civil War* (1965), pp. 110, 128. George Orwell, who arrived in Spain in December 1936, and enrolled in the POUM militia on the Aragon front, does not mention the question of arms in his account (*Homage to Catalonia*, 1938).

4
CHINKS IN THE DEFENCES

In the spring of 1937, relations between Largo Caballero and the PCE, never easy, began to deteriorate rapidly. Being Minister of Defence as well as Prime Minister, he took the full brunt of responsibility for military reverses. The first attacks on him took the form of criticism of generals whom he was known to favour. He was said to support the old professional "non-party" officers who sought to impede the creation of a unified "people's army" on the pretext that this would bring the army under direct party control. He began to show mistrust of the international brigades, whose strong revolutionary and party complexion made them recalcitrant to professional control. In January 1937, he attempted to limit recruitment to them, and in April to liquidate their central headquarters at Albacete.[1] He was jealous of the growing activity of the military commissars, and on April 14, 1937, issued a decree the effect of which would have been to subordinate them to the control of the Ministry of Defence.[2] Friction occurred in other spheres. The opposition of Largo Caballero proved fatal to negotiations for the unification of the PCE and PSOE; he is said to have told Codovilla that communists who desired unity had only to join the PSOE and the UGT.[3] Angered by Díaz's attack on the government at the session of the central committee of the PCE, he wrote a letter to Díaz calling for the resignation of Hernández, the communist Minister for Public Education, whose "tactless" speech at the session had been "incompatible with the post occupied by him".[4] Pressure from the PCE, now that communist trade unions had merged with the UGT, for communist representation in the council of the UGT, was stubbornly resisted by Largo Caballero, who rightly feared attempts to undermine his authority.[5] He seems to have drawn

---

[1] M. Meshcheryakov, *Ispanskaya Respublika i Komintern* (1981), p. 107.

[2] *Ibid.* pp. 67–69.

[3] *Ibid.* p. 79, according to Largo Caballero's memoirs written many years later, which may have exaggerated his intransigence.

[4] M. Meshcheryakov, *Ispanskaya Respublika i Komintern* (1981), p. 81.

[5] D. Cattell, *Communism and the Spanish Civil War* (1965), p. 123.

nearer at this time to his old opponent in the PSOE, Prieto, and indulged freely in complaints of "communist intrigues" and "orders from Moscow".[6] He promoted a scheme for substituting a government representing the trade unions for the government representing parties, which failed to win the approval of his colleagues in the PSOE.[7] If the story of a plot hatched by him to end the war by an offer of bases in Spain to Italy, and of mining rights to Germany, in return for the exclusion of Soviet influence, has any foundation, it would fully account for the growing communist animosity towards him.[8]

Throughout the spring of 1937 the military situation remained tense. The loss of Málaga in February was balanced by a victory over Franco's Italian allies at Guadalajara on the outskirts of Madrid in March, the first positive achievement of the people's army. But at the end of March Franco launched a new offensive against the Basque region in the north, with the port of Bilbao as its final objective. The Spanish Basques, though strongly Catholic, had a tradition of hostility to the Spanish monarchy, which rejected their claim to autonomy, and were fiercely opposed to Franco. On October 1, 1936, the reconstituted republican government passed a decree recognizing the right of the Basques to autonomy, and an autonomous Basque Government was set up.[9] But this step hindered rather than helped the integration of the Basque armed units into the republican people's army; and they were poorly supplied with tanks, aeroplanes and other military equipment. While the army of the insurgents advanced slowly by land, their navy blockaded Bilbao.

---

[6] J. Martín Blázquez, *I Helped to Build an Army* (1939), p. 319; the writer was a friend of Prieto.

[7] *Guerra y Revolución en España*, iii (Moscow, 1971), 60–61.

[8] H. Thomas, *The Spanish Civil War* (3rd edn, 1977), p. 650; but this story, like the anecdote of a quarrel between Largo Caballero and Álvarez del Vayo about the latter's subservience to Soviet advice (*ibid.* pp. 533–534) is highly suspect. As commonly happens after a military stalemate, rumours of overtures for a negotiated peace abounded on all sides in the spring of 1937. Largo Caballero certainly indulged in such talk; according to S. Payne (*The Spanish Revolution* [1970], pp. 271–272) the unpublished papers of Araquistáin, the Spanish Ambassador in Paris, contain piquant details. For a confused account of alleged negotiations about Morocco, in which Largo Caballero and the French and British governments were all involved, see J. Hernández, *La Grande Trahison* (1953), pp. 63–64.

[9] *Kommunisticheskii Internatsional*, No. 17 (1936), pp. 105–106.

The bombing by German aircraft of Guernica, the old Basque capital and now a small undefended town, became the most notorious incident of the war, and provoked an outburst of indignation against the rebels in many countries. But the loss of the Basque territory and of access to the Biscay coast was a serious blow to the republicans, and brought the political crisis to a head.

No open attack had been made on Largo Caballero at the session of the Central Committee on March 4-5, 1937. But, according to a highly coloured account published twenty years later by Hernández, the conference was followed by a secret party meeting attended by Codovilla, Stepanov, a member of the Comintern secretariat, and Marty, at which the proposal was made to remove Largo Caballero, and look for an alternative Prime Minister. Heated discussion followed. But only Díaz and Hernández voted against the proposal; and Díaz declared himself ready to accept the view of the majority.[10] Some such meeting may well have taken place, but the details of this version are probably fictitious. Hernández names Togliatti among those present. But Togliatti, on his own showing, did not come to Spain till July 1937, and other evidence conclusively supports him.[11] It is doubtful whether any firm decision was taken at this time.

Ever since the fall of Málaga in February 1937, constant re-criminations about Largo Caballero's conduct of military affairs showed that he had lost the confidence of the communists and of their Soviet mentors. A serious bone of contention was the rivalry between the Ministry of Defence, which sought to maintain the principles of the old professional army, and the new commissariat of military commissars, which served the PCE and the Soviet advisers as a main channel of contact with the government on the

[10] J. Hernández, *La Grande Trahison* (1953), pp. 54-58.

[11] P. Spriano, *Storia del Partito Comunista Italiano*, iii (1970), 215. Marty wrote an article in the latter part of March 1937, which called Largo Caballero "the courageous leader of the Spanish government" and contained no hint of criticism (*Rundschau*, No. 14, April 1, 1937, p. 534). I. Ehrenburg, *Eve of War* (Engl. trans., 1963), p. 167, describes Marty during his visit to Valencia in the spring of 1937 as "imperious, very short-tempered, always suspecting everyone of treason,...like a mentally sick man". According to Cogniot, a member of the central committee of the PCF, who claims to have been present, IKKI desired to keep Marty in Moscow, but Marty reacted so furiously against the proposal that, after spending a whole night arguing with Dimitrov, he "unfortunately" got his way and was allowed to go to Spain (C. Willard *et al.*, *Le Front Populaire* [1972], p. 137). The incident is not precisely dated.

army and on military policy. A conference of military commissars from all fronts was held in Albacete on April 2, 1937. It was addressed by Álvarez del Vayo and Miaja on behalf of the general commissariat, and those attending included 20 socialists, 16 communists and 3 anarchists. The resolutions adopted by the conference appear to have contained nothing new. But the purpose of the exercise was clearly to enhance the authority and influence of the military commissars and of the commissariat.[12] Largo Caballero accepted the challenge, and on April 14 issued an order on the reorganization of the commissariat, which, in the words of a commentator, "practically annulled the decisions of the conference, and abolished the whole system of organization and ideology established over the past half year by the efforts of the commissars and the commissariat". It was clearly designed to place the commissariat under the control of the ministry, and contained a provision that any commissar who had not been confirmed in his post by May 15, in the official gazette, should be regarded as dismissed.[13] The order was certainly unenforceable. But it was a declaration of war which brought the conflict to a flash-point.

The crisis which proved fatal to Largo Caballero flared up in Barcelona. The anarchists were stronger in Catalonia than elsewhere in Spain, and POUM was almost exclusively Catalan. The CNT and POUM on one side were confronted on the other by forces of the Moscow-backed government and the substantially communist PSUC, both now determined to exert their authority to the full. An explosion could hardly be avoided. The operators who controlled the Barcelona telephone exchange were faithful members of CNT unions, and interfered, or were suspected of interfering, with official communications between Barcelona and Valencia or Madrid. On May 3, 1937, government troops attempted to take over the building. Resistance was greater than had been expected. Anarchists and supporters of POUM rose in revolt all over the city, and street fighting continued for two or three days, with many casualties. The cause of the insurgents was rendered hopeless by a split in the CNT. In a desperate military situation, a majority of the leaders yielded to the argument that discipline and unity in the republican army were required if

---

[12] *Pod Znamenem Ispanskoi Respubliki* (1965), pp. 242–248.
[13] *Ibid*. pp. 430, 435–437.

Franco's armies were to be beaten off, and came out against the revolt. Defeat of the insurgents was followed by the usual quota of arrests and executions, and order was restored. The PSUC, in a carefully worded statement, placed the main responsibility for resisting "the organization of an anti-Fascist victory" on the Trotskyites, identified as "the leaders of POUM", whose methods were denounced as "conscious lying, conscious provocation, conscious support for Fascism". Next to them came the "uncontrollables", socially rootless people who had "worked their way into anarchist workers' organizations", and who now accused the CNT leaders of treachery. The government was preparing to take energetic measures against them. "The Trotskyites" and "uncontrollables" and other "provocateurs" had seen their last salvation in open revolt.[14]

The Barcelona rising placed Largo Caballero in an impossible situation. As secretary-general of the UGT, he had always posed as a good revolutionary, associated with the Left wing of the PSOE. The progressive shift to the Right in communist policy cannot have been congenial to him; and both the strength and the weakness of his character were incompatible with docile subservience to a party line. In the Barcelona affair, he had been responsible as Prime Minister for actions which he neither directed nor controlled, and about which his personal sympathies were ambivalent. Díaz repeated the official diagnosis at a mass meeting in Valencia on May 9, 1937. He celebrated the achievement of the PCE and of the popular front; a tribute to General Miaja was greeted with an ovation. Preaching caution in domestic policy, he issued a warning against attempts by "committees" to control factories, and by "groups" and "organizations" to take over the land. He denounced Trotskyites as agents of Fascism, and held them responsible for the "criminal putsch" in Barcelona. He did not name POUM, but censured its paper *La Batalla* for instigating the disturbances. He denied any hostility towards the CNT; it would not be fair to blame the organization for what was done by "uncontrolled" elements. He ended with a plea for the unification of the parties of the Left, and for the

---

[14] *Rundschau*, No. 22, May 20, 1937, pp. 809–810; Franco assured the German ambassador that "the street fighting [in Barcelona] had been started by his agents" – an implausible claim (*Akten zur Deutschen Auswärtigen Politik*, Serie D, iii [1951], 243).

creation by the UGT and the CNT of a unified trade union centre. But the tone was sharp. Díaz did not attack Largo Caballero by name. But he issued a warning that, if the government did not pursue a "firm policy", this would have to be done by "another government of the popular front".[15] The crisis came when, at a cabinet meeting on May 15, 1937, Largo Caballero resisted a communist proposal to outlaw POUM and to reduce anarchist representation in the government. The communist members left the meeting in disgust, and on the following day, Largo Caballero handed in his resignation to Azaña.[16]

The rapidity with which a new government was formed suggests that the ground had been well prepared. On May 17, 1937, the Finance Minister, Negrín, took office as Prime Minister in a government which excluded the anarchists as well as POUM. The campaign against Largo Caballero was pursued with undiminished vigour.[17] Negrín himself belonged to the Right of the PSOE, and was a friend of Prieto, who retained his post as Minister for Defence. Álvarez del Vayo, who had been a close associate of Largo Caballero, suffered a partial eclipse. He was succeeded as Foreign Minister by Giral, the former Prime Minister and a moderate republican, but was allowed to retain his appointment as Spanish delegate to the League of Nations. The PCE issued a statement promising to support any popular front government which would ensure the devotion of all "human and material elements in the country" to a victory which would open the way for "our people's revolution", and expressing in particular the wish "to go hand in hand with our comrades of the CNT".[18] The tactical objective of the Comintern and the Soviet government at this time was to exercise control over Spanish affairs through friendly or docile members of other Spanish

[15] J. Díaz, *Tres Años de Lucha* (Paris, 1970), pp. 422–443; an abbreviated version appeared in *Kommunisticheskii Internatsional*, No. 5 (1937), pp. 62–71.

[16] D. Cattell, *Communism and the Spanish Civil War* (1965), pp. 155–156. The account of the meeting came from Largo Caballero himself and his supporter Araquistáin; for a detailed record of the crisis see *Guerra y Revolución en España*, iii (Moscow, 1971), 79–83.

[17] Hernández, as spokesman of the PCE, delivered a long and scathing indictment at a public meeting in Valencia (the text, published in *Frente Rojo*, May 29, 31, 1937, appears in *Ispanskaya Kompartiya Borot'sya za Pobedu* [1939], pp. 79–101); Ibárruri's speech introducing Hernández to the audience is in D. Ibárruri, *Speeches and Articles* (1978), pp. 94–98.

[18] *Rundschau*, No. 22, May 20, 1937, pp. 798–799.

parties. The two communist ministers remained, but their number was not increased. To assign too conspicuous a role to the PCE would have been liable both to alienate moderate Spanish opinion and to alarm those political circles in France and Britain which the Soviet government was expressly anxious to propitiate. The moderate complexion of the new government, shorn of every overtly revolutionary element, reflected this design. The first declaration of the Negrín government spoke the language of democracy, and promised, through the agency of the popular front, to crush the rebellion and maintain the independence of Spain.[19] Negrín was a competent administrator, without strong political convictions or ambitions. He was, from the point of view of Moscow, an excellent choice. But he was no revolutionary. A representative of the British ILP in Spain, sympathetic to the views of POUM, observed bitterly that Comintern "does not want to see a Red Spain any more than it wants to see a Fascist Spain".[20]

The PSUC and the government in Barcelona were now strong enough to complete their victory over those responsible for the May insurrection. At the end of May, a conference of the UGT, doubtless under some pressure, was induced by a majority of 24 to 14 to declare its support for the Negrín government.[21] The ranks of the anarchist CNT had been split by the rising. Its leadership had come to recognize that the defence of the republic called imperatively for common action by all republican forces, and a temporary postponement of far-reaching revolutionary designs. The CNT adopted a programme which was said "to correspond in the main to communist demands". It stressed the need for unified political leadership and military command, for a plan to rebuild the economy, and for common ownership of the land, with the proviso that peasants should be free to cultivate it either individually or collectively.[22] The full fury of the authorities, with the tacit connivance of the CNT, fell on POUM.

On May 28, 1937, the journal *La Batalla* was banned. On June 16, POUM was outlawed by decree, its premises were seized, and no known members of it were safe from arrest. Nin disappeared,

[19] *Guerra y Revolución en España*, iii (Moscow, 1971), 87–88.
[20] *New Leader*, May 28, 1937.
[21] *Guerra y Revolución en España*, iii (Moscow, 1971), 97–98.
[22] *Rundschau*, No. 25, June 10, 1937, p. 904.

and was never heard of again; he was probably killed – it was said, after torture – by the army or the police. The remaining POUM battalions at the front were disbanded or merged with other units.

This savage victimization of POUM seems to have been the signal for the creation in the summer of 1937 of a new body whose professed function was counter-espionage, the Servicio de Investigación Militar (SIM). This organization quickly spread its tentacles to all parts of republican Spain, occupying itself with the suppression of all forms of opposition, and employing the familiar instruments of imprisonment, investigation and torture. These proceedings provoked a wave of indignation among supporters of the Left in Western countries. For the first time, a body of opinion arose which, while implacably hostile to Franco, was sharply critical of the suppression of dissidents of the Left in Spain. The comparison with the purges in the USSR, now at their height, was freely cited; and what was happening in Spain was attributed to the Soviet advisers and agents.

When the central committee of the PCE met on June 18–21, 1937, the party seemed well placed to outstrip and absorb its rivals and to assume the dominant position in the affairs of the republic. The main item on the agenda was an appeal for a single united party of the proletariat and for the popular front. Díaz was absent, ill, and Ibárruri, who made the main report, delivered an eloquent call for the unity of the working class, including an appeal for joint action between the UGT and the CNT. Comorera, the secretary of the Catalan PSUC, and Santiago Carrillo, the secretary of the united communist and socialist youth organizations, praised contributions made by their respective organizations to the cause of unity. The resolution instructed the party politburo to submit to the PSOE for discussion a document which would lay "the programmatic and tactical foundation" for unity; and the call for unity was endorsed by a mass meeting of 60,000 workers in Madrid.[23] The session was marked by a mood of self-congratulation which took little account of the grim realities of the situation.

---

[23] *Kommunisticheskiï Internatsional*, No. 7 (1937), pp. 49–66; for Ibárruri's report, which was published in *Frente Rojo*, June 21, 1937, see D. Ibárruri, *Speeches and Articles* (1978), pp. 99–122. The session also discussed party work in the army (see p. 59 below).

◻5◻
CALCULATIONS OF DIPLOMACY

The replacement of Largo Caballero by Negrín as Prime Minister could be read as a turning-point in the history of the Spanish republic and of the civil war. It symbolized a reversal of priorities. Largo Caballero was an impulsive revolutionary demagogue, the popular leader of the Left wing of the PSOE. Negrín was a cautious administrator and disciplinarian, a member of the Centre or Right of the PSOE; and this made him an acceptable head of government for the PCE, from whose programme revolutionary elements had been carefully expunged, and which demanded only efficiency in the conduct of the war. Here Negrín's appointment marked a certain advance. For the first time the army had been unified. One of the first decrees of the new government, on May 27, 1937, provided for a reorganization of the armed forces under the control of the Ministry of Defence. A week later Negrín established a Supreme War Council, consisting of himself, Prieto, a socialist, Giral, a republican, and Uribe, a communist, to oversee the conduct of hostilities – a token of the broad popular front.[1] Political unity had been achieved under the dominant activity of the PCE, POUM had been annihilated, and the anarchists called to order by their own leaders. The creation of SIM as a special department for the defence of the state was proof of a new determination to combat espionage and the "fifth column".[2]

Something had been gained. But much also had been lost. The spontaneous revolutionary ardour, ill-organized and ill-coordinated though it was, which animated the republican armies in the first autumn and winter of the war, gave place to a dour defensive struggle to avert disaster, which discouraged any visionary hopes or ambitions for the future. The revolutionaries of many nations who had marched to the defence of Madrid in November 1936 found no corresponding inspiration in the

[1] *Guerra y Revolución en España*, iii (Moscow, 1971), 88–89.
[2] *Ibid.* iii, 89.

defence of Azaña's bourgeois republic. The fortunes of war fluctuated. In July 1937, by way of compensation for their losses in the north, the republicans in a desperate battle – the so-called battle of Brunete – succeeded in breaking through the close ring with which the rebel forces enveloped Madrid. But by this time the people's army was fighting with its back to the wall. Catalonia and Valencia still held firm, with Madrid and its environs representing a broad salient projecting into enemy terrain. But two-thirds of the territory was in the hands of Franco and his allies. Talk of a negotiated peace, which had been in the air since the spring, now took more definite form, and was widely attributed to Prieto himself.[3] A mood of fatalism crept over the Spanish Left. Hopes of victory were relegated far into the future.

The interest of the international Left in the Spanish civil war, and enthusiasm for the republic in its ordeal, so vividly kindled during the first winter of the war, had also lost its novelty and some of its attraction by the summer of 1937. On March 9–10, 1937, a few days after the session of the central committee of the PCE in Valencia,[4] the Second and Amsterdam Internationals held a conference in London, attended by 200 delegates and presided over by Citrine. The conference originated in a proposal of the PSOE and UGT for a comprehensive conference of all anti-Fascist organizations to consider ways and means of coming to the aid of the Spanish republic; this proposal had been unhesitatingly rejected by the leaders of the two Internationals, who were determined to confine the proceedings to their own members. A manifesto addressed to the conference by the CPGB was pointedly ignored. The Spanish delegation, having expressed disappointment at the restricted composition of the gathering, proposed that governments should withdraw from the now wholly one-sided non-intervention agreement, that arms and munitions should be supplied to the Spanish government, and that "a simultaneous and complete stoppage of work" should be organized by workers in Western countries in protest against the attitude of

[3] Franco spoke to the German ambassador in Salamanca on May 23, 1937, of proposals for a truce, which was quite unacceptable to him, and remarked that "the whole action started from Prieto", who had visited Blum in Paris, and hoped for mediation by the French or United States governments (*Akten zur Deutschen Auswärtigen Politik*, Serie D, iii [1951], 249); for earlier talk attributed to Largo Caballero, see p. 38, n. 8 above.

[4] See p. 39 above.

their governments. The French delegates approved the stoppage of work in principle, but doubted its favourable effect on governments or on public opinion. Nobody else had anything to say for it. The British delegates were concerned to deplore "the continual attempts to secure an all-in conference, which had the effect of diverting attention from the real issue of helping Spain, and concentrating it on the controversial issue of the 'united front'". It was pointed out that no one had suggested that the democratic powers should intervene. A long resolution at the conclusion of the conference was full of eloquent verbal protests, and proposed no action whatever.[5]

The pristine revolutionary enthusiasm for the Spanish republic was now maintained in Britain primarily by the ILP. The role of the British delegation at the conference of the Internationals was denounced in scathing terms in the ILP journal. The Spanish delegation had been "broken more by Bevin than by Franco"; and Bevin's "brutal" speech had shown him as worse than de Brouckère and Vandervelde.[6] A conference of the ILP at the end of March 1937 had the Spanish question as its background. But, since the Spanish delegation at the conference came from POUM, the views propounded by it were anathema to the CPGB and PCE and to the Spanish government, no less than to the Second International and the British Government.[7]

A dramatic incident which occurred at this time illustrated the cautious mood prevailing in the leadership of the PCE, as well as the mutual suspicion and incompatibility of purpose which divided the socialist and communist parties of western Europe, and the two Internationals. Naval engagements were at this time normally avoided by both sides. But on May 31, under what provocation never became clear, a squadron of republican aviators dropped a number of bombs on the German cruiser *Deutschland*, causing 80 casualties. Reprisals were called for; and on the night

---

[5] *Trades Union Congress: Sixty-Ninth Annual Report* (1937), pp. 174–175; *Report of the Thirty-Seventh Annual Conference of the Labour Party* (1937), pp. 8–10. Only the latter account prints the text of the resolution, and discloses the fact that the Spanish delegation, disillusioned by its anodyne character, abstained from voting on it; for the CPGB manifesto see *Rundschau*, No. 11, March 11, 1937, p. 437.

[6] *New Leader*, March 19, 1937.

[7] *Ibid.* April 2, 1937.

of May 31, 1937, the German fleet bombarded the coastal town of Almería, destroying houses and killing a number of civilians.[8] This brutal act caused a sharp division in the government. Prieto, as Minister of Defence, proposed to mount a systematic attack by the air force on German warships in the Mediterranean. The other members of the government resisted and temporized. Negrín proposed to seek the advice of Azaña, the communist ministers to consult the central committee of the PCE. Prieto's dangerous gesture found no support.[9] An article by Dimitrov in the Comintern journal denounced this "open, shameless act of war", and argued that "an enormous historical responsibility" rested on the Second International for keeping the workers' movements divided. The article contained, however, no hint of military action to avenge the attack.[10]

Where deeds were lacking, eloquent words took their place. On June 1 the PCE and the PSOE sent identical telegrams to the Second International, the Communist International and the Amsterdam International, protesting against this "revolting act of barbarism" and calling for "international proletarian solidarity" to resist "the plans of Fascism, which wishes to plunge the world into the hell of a world war". Dimitrov sent an appropriately enthusiastic reply, and followed this up with a telegram to de Brouckère, proposing to establish a "coordinating commission" of the three Internationals to organize common action. De Brouckère on June 7 took refuge in a formal objection: neither the president nor the secretary of the International was empowered to accept such an invitation. Two days later, Dimitrov came back with another eloquent appeal, ending with a plea for a "preliminary" meeting between representatives of the two Internationals. This time de Brouckère acquiesced. Thorez, Cachin, Díaz, Dahlem and Longo were nominated to represent Comintern at the meeting, which took place at Annemasse on June 21. Togliatti, though not a delegate, arrived from Moscow in time to participate in the proceedings. De Brouckère and Adler

[8] For a full account of this episode see *Pod Znamenem Ispanskoi Respubliki* (1965), pp. 253–255.

[9] Prieto's attitude is recorded in his memoirs, H. Thomas, *The Spanish Civil War* (3rd edn, 1977), p. 586; the story that Prieto's proposal was vetoed on instructions from Moscow (J. Hernández, *La Grande Trahison* [1953], p. 95) will not hold water; there was no time for such consultation. The introduction of Togliatti into the story is also an anachronism.

[10] *Kommunisticheskii Internatsional*, No. 6 (1937), pp. 9–12.

once again represented the Second International.[11]

The joint communiqué at the end of the meeting recorded the support of both Internationals for the removal of the blockade, the re-establishment in Spain of international law violated by the Fascists, and the application of the Covenant of the League of Nations, and proposed "a more detailed study" on a further occasion in the near future of ways and means of rendering moral and material aid to the Spanish republic.[12] A conference of the Second and Amsterdam Internationals in Paris on June 24 once more expressed sympathy with the Spanish republic and indignation at the Fascist aggression of Italy and Germany, invoked the Covenant of the League of Nations, and protested against the indifference of the Western governments.[13] It was apparently on this occasion that de Brouckère, according to Togliatti, "caused a great stir" and offered to go to Moscow "to meet Stalin", but failed to shake the apathy of a deeply divided International.[14]

The future meeting projected at the Annemasse conference took place on July 9. On the eve of the meeting Togliatti, in a confidential report to Moscow, repeated his diagnosis of the crisis in the Second International and warned IKKI against the assumption that, as a result of the Annemasse conference, "reactionary elements in the Second International, enemies of the united front", are much weakened.[15] The meeting of July 9 ended with a communiqué recording "the common agreement of both Internationals on the actions necessary for the benefit of republican Spain".[16] But no such actions followed. Togliatti wearily detected "a certain tiredness" in the Western communist parties; demonstrations in support of Spain no longer drew mass participation.[17] Dimitrov, in an article in *Pravda*, ostensibly

[11] According to M. Meshcheryakov, *Ispanskaya Respublika i Komintern* (1971), Thorez failed to make the journey, the French delegation being headed by Bonté; Díaz, absent through illness (see p. 44 above), was replaced by Checa (*Guerra y Revolución en España*, iii [Moscow, 1971], 222–223).

[12] *Kommunisticheskii Internatsional*, No. 6 (1937), pp. 113–123.

[13] *Trades Union Congress: Sixty-Ninth Annual Report* (1937), p. 177; *Report of the Thirty-Seventh Annual Conference of the Labour Party* (1937), pp. 11–12.

[14] P. Togliatti, *Opere*, IV, i (1979), p. 254; see Note B, pp. 89–90 below.

[15] *Ibid.* pp. 254–255.

[16] *Kommunisticheskii Internatsional*, No. 7 (1937), p. 16.

[17] P. Togliatti, *Opere*, IV, i (1979), p. 255.

designed to correct an excessive reliance on leaders, appealed to the workers of all countries for unity in order to "fulfil their duty to the Spanish people".[18] But such exhortations, constantly repeated, failed more and more patently to mask the luke-warmness of the response; and these exchanges resembled a ritual dance whose original meaning had been blunted by long usage and constant repetition. The British government took less and less trouble to conceal its indifference to the fate of the republic. The British Ambassador, together with his French and United States colleagues, established himself comfortably at Saint Jean-de-Luz, leaving a junior diplomat in charge of the Embassy in Madrid. Chamberlain, in his first statement on the subject as Prime Minister, in the House of Commons on June 25, 1937, pointedly refrained from any expression of sympathy or support for the Spanish republican government, and explained that British policy was directed "to one end, and to one end only, namely, to maintain the peace of Europe by confining the war to Spain".[19]

However, behind these undeniable symptoms in the Western world of a waning emotional involvement in the agony of the Spanish republic, the more insidious question presented itself of attitudes and policies in the USSR. Outwardly nothing changed. Well-known assurances of sympathy and support were depicted with undiminished eloquence. Familiar gestures were renewed. Military supplies and equipment, though less lavish than those received by Franco from his allies, continued to reach the republican forces. But the summer of 1937 was marked in Moscow, as in the West, by an unconfessed weakening of interest. The revolutionary ardour so easily whipped up in the summer and autumn of 1936 to fire the struggle against Fascism, had given place to the cool calculations of diplomacy; Spain was a pawn on the European chess-board.[20] Perhaps the hitherto unthinkable prospect of a defeat of the republic by Franco's

---

[18] *Pravda*, July 18, 1937.

[19] *House of Commons: Fifth Series*, CCCXXV (1937), 1545–1550.

[20] Trotsky's attitude was also complex; while in theory he dismissed the popular front as a device for keeping the revolution within bourgeois-democratic limits, and preventing a confrontation between Franco's capitalist regime and a proletarian revolution to overthrow capitalism, he recognized in practice that "the Negrín–Stalin government is a quasi-democratic brake on the road to socialism, but is also a brake, surely neither certain nor durable, but neverthe-less a brake, on the road to Fascism". For the moment, "the military struggle

victorious allies had begun, in the inner military councils of the USSR, to seem less unrealistic.

Nor was the wider outlook, as seen from Moscow, any more reassuring. The German–Italian axis, cemented by cooperation in Spain, and now reinforced by the enigmatic power of Japan, more directly menacing to the USSR than to Europe, boldly confronted the shifting and hesitant policies of France and Britain, and, somewhere in the background, that sprawling and indecisive colossus, the United States of America. Whatever other significance could be read into Stalin's purge of the generals in June 1937, it indicated a deep unease in foreign policy; Tukhachevsky had been a conspicuous protagonist of the anti-Fascist front.[21] The whole conception had come to wear a hollow look. The time had not yet come to formulate, or even to admit, the possibility of any alternative policy to confront the German menace. But the unspoken recognition that some other way might some day have to be found imparted a certain irresolution to the implementation of existing policies, in Spain and elsewhere.[22]

---

between Negrín and Franco continues, and today's tactics are dictated by today's situation" (L. Trotsky, *Écrits, 1928–1940*, iii [1959], pp. 528–530).

[21] Blükher, who survived the Tukhachevsky purge, but met the same fate a year later, played a similar role in the East.

[22] According to apparently unpublished memoirs of Orlov, quoted in S. Payne, *The Spanish Revolution* (1970), p. 274, "instructions were sent in the summer of 1937 that Soviet policy would no longer be to provide the large-scale assistance calculated to secure an all-out victory, but to extend the struggle on a long-term basis keeping the Leftist forces in the field as long as possible, and so denying complete victory to the nationalists". In the absence of documents, what the NKVD in Moscow may have written to its representatives abroad is guess-work. But it is unlikely that any formal decision was taken at party or government levels; what happened at most was a change of emphasis and priorities.

⌈6⌉
"DEMOCRACY OF A NEW TYPE"

Consciousness of the precarious situation in Spain, and of the new problems and dangers facing Negrín's government, evidently prompted a decision by Comintern to send to Spain on a mission of enquiry its most experienced foreign co-adjutor. During the past year, Togliatti, however cautious his official utterances, had been fully convinced that the revolution, in countries like Italy and Spain, was still in its bourgeois-democratic phase. The first stage of the struggle against Fascism must be for a new type of democracy. Emphasis should fall on the struggle between democracy and Fascism.[1] Before leaving Moscow he had a conversation with Dimitrov, and an identity of views was established between them.[2] He arrived in Annemasse in time to attend the conference there on June 21–22, 1937,[3] and went on to Valencia, where he remained for almost three months, reporting periodically to Moscow on problems and prospects.[4] His code name in the PCE was Alfredo, and he held credentials as correspondent of the Paris newspaper *Le Soir*.[5]

Togliatti's conclusions, when he summed them up at the end of August 1937, were neither flattering nor encouraging. Negrín was better than Largo Caballero. But the government did not have sufficient contacts with the population. Its language was pedestrian, "cold and bureaucratic"; it was unable to "stimulate popular enthusiasm, and thus transform the war into a war of the whole nation against the aggressor". The danger was that its feebleness tended to "create a bloc of opposition to the govern-

[1] See his conversations with Bibolotti, reported in P. Spriano, *Storia del Partito Comunista Italiano*, iii (1970), pp. 53–61.
[2] *Georgii Dimitrov: Vydayushchiisya Deyatel' Kommunisticheskogo Dvizheniya* (1972), p. 348.
[3] See p. 48 above.
[4] P. Togliatti, *Opere*, IV, i (1979), 253–279, contains reports of July 8 and August 30 to IKKI, and a letter to Dimitrov and Manuilsky of September 15; doubtless there were others; see Note B, pp. 89–98 below.
[5] M. Meshcheryakov, *Ispanskaya Respublika i Komintern* (1981), p. 115.

ment which is also a bloc of fierce enemies of the PCE" – a bloc including Trotskyites and anarchists, who denounced Negrín's regime as counter-revolutionary. Togliatti's conventional praise of the PCE thinly veiled sharp criticisms. Weaknesses were attributed to rapid growth and lack of experienced cadres. The central committee and the politburo were ill-organized, and policy was often indecisive and incoherent.[6]

The proceedings of the central committee of the PCE in June 1937 had been dominated by proposals for the fusion of the PSOE with the PCE into a single proletarian party.[7] Profound enthusiasm in the PCE was, however, thwarted by "sharp swings" of opinion in a divided PSOE. Largo Caballero's hostility to the PCE was now implacable; and he still wielded influence in the UGT. Recriminations abounded. The communist journal *Frente Rojo* described the executive committee of the UGT as "a group of people hostile to unity, hostile to the nation, bankrupt and embittered, who rate their bitterness and personal passions above the sacred interest of the nation". Largo Caballero refused to attend a meeting summoned to discuss a PCE draft; and the politburo of the PCE, in a solemn resolution of July 19, deplored "the negative attitude of a majority of members of the executive committee of the UGT".[8] It now became imperative, if further progress was to be made, to shake Largo Caballero's remaining bastion of power as president of the UGT. On September 4, 1937, the joint committee of the PCE and the PSOE called for the early convocation of the executive committee of the UGT.[9] Relations were patched up sufficiently to allow a joint committee of the two parties to draft a programme of common action, which was published in the party journals of August 19 and 20. It envisaged joint action in promoting greater efficiency in the army, in war production and in "the coordination and planning of the economy", as well as "good relations with the industrial and commercial petty bourgeoisie". It called for the strengthening of the popular front, and of unity between the two parties in the trade unions, in the youth organization, and in

[6] P. Togliatti, *Opere*, IV, i, (1979), 258–272; see Note B, pp. 91–94 below.
[7] See p. 44 above.
[8] *Kommunisticheskii Internatsional*, No. 8 (1937), p. 78; M. Meshcheryakov, *Ispanskaya Respublika i Komintern* (1981), pp. 90–91.
[9] Ibid. p. 124.

international relations; and it ended with a commitment to the defence of the USSR and to its struggle "against international Fascism, for democracy and freedom of peoples".[10] It was a document of eloquent words and no great practical content. Its shortcomings were emphasized in an enigmatic resolution recorded by the chief PSOE delegate at the moment of signature. It was simply a programme of unity of action, not for the "organized fusion" of the parties into what the Spanish proletariat so much disliked: a single workers' party.[11] Togliatti in his report of August 30 remarked on continual opposition in the PSOE,[12] and nobody seems to have taken the prospect of fusion very seriously.

Relations with the anarchists were more significant, and caused more anxiety to the PCE, than relations with the socialists. The interlude of warmly expressed friendship in the last month of 1936[13] scarcely lasted into 1937; and the May rising in Barcelona, when anarchists provided the hard core of resistance to the government and came near to overturning it, led to bitter recriminations. The PCE could not, however, afford a break. On May 17, the day of the formation of Negrín's government, it issued a manifesto declaring its willingness to go "hand in hand as united brothers with our comrades of the CNT, and together with them struggle for victory".[14] The appeal had a mixed reception. Many CNT unions showed outspoken sympathy for Largo Caballero. But the leaders of the CNT had also been uneasy at developments which could only bring aid and support to Franco, and disowned their unruly followers. At the beginning of July 1937, the political arm of the anarchist movement, the hitherto not very active Iberian Anarchist Federation (FAI), decided at a conference in Valencia to organize its activities and convert itself into a political party, thus implying acceptance of the legitimacy of the state. In response to an overture from the PCE, a meeting between representatives of the PCE and of the CNT and the FAI concluded on August 15 an agreement for joint action "at the front and the rear", and for the cessation of polemics in the press if this implied the suppression of "uncontrollable elements" in the

---

[10] *Guerra y Revolución en España*, iii (Moscow, 1971), 210–217.

[11] D. Cattell, *Communism and the Spanish Civil War* (1965), pp. 181–182.

[12] P. Togliatti, *Opere*, IV, i (1979), 268.

[13] See pp. 31–34 above.

[14] D. Cattell, *Communism and the Spanish Civil War* (1965), p. 241, note 2.

anarchist camp. Unfortunately, on the following day, the Negrín government, probably ignorant of these negotiations, saw fit to dissolve the council of the Aragon province, which was controlled by anarchists; and this high-handed action so infuriated the anarchist negotiators that relations were broken off.[15] Togliatti, in his initial report of July 8, merely recommended a conciliatory approach to the anarchists in order to bring them into the government. But when he wrote on August 30, he had become alive to the perplexities of the situation. The government had been inept in its handling of the anarchists. But the FAI, together with the "Trotskyites", had denounced the government as counter-revolutionary, and called for an insurrection to overthrow it.[16] No other country except Spain presented this baffling complication of powerful anarchist movements, equally hostile to capitalism and communism, and commanding the allegiance of a large body, perhaps a preponderance, of the workers.

In Catalonia the fissiparous tendencies of the past had still not been overcome. A new government of the Generalitat was formed in the summer of 1937 by an alliance between communists and Catalan nationalists at the expense of the anarchist CNT. The PSUC, formed a year earlier to cement an alliance between communists and socialists in Catalonia,[17] held a "national conference" in July, which revealed an enormous increase in its numbers, but no great homogeneity in the elements out of which it was composed.[18] The politburo of the PCE, at a meeting on July 30, was able to congratulate itself. The PSUC had grown in numbers and in organization, and had become "one of the decisive forces in the Catalan anti-Fascist bloc, a factor in the stubborn struggle to defend the national and social interests of the Catalan people, and in the efforts necessary to gain victory in alliance with the Spanish people". On the other hand, it lamented that the pact between the UGT and the CNT had yielded no practical results.[19] The general assembly of the

---

[15] M. Meshcheryakov, *Ispanskaya Respublika i Komintern* (1981), p. 116; for the Valencia conference of the FAI see also S. Payne, *The Spanish Revolution* (1970), p. 303.

[16] P. Togliatti, *Opere*, IV, i (1979), 268.

[17] See p. 31 above.

[18] M. Meshcheryakov, *Ispanskaya Respublika i Komintern* (1981), pp. 131–132.

[19] *Kommunisticheskii Internatsional*, No. 8 (1937), pp. 79–80; for the pact

Generalitat met on August 19, apparently for the first time since the beginning of the war, but failed to resolve the dilemma and adjourned *sine die*.[20] The problem of Catalan nationalism, with the problem of anarchism, remained a thorn in the side of communists eager to place themselves at the head of a united Spanish national movement against the Fascists.

The economic policy of the Negrín government was concerned to curb and reverse revolutionary measures taken in the first flush of enthusiasm in the early days of the war. The taking over of factories and their management by committees of workers had been accompanied by the widespread phenomenon of falling production. On June 16, 1937, the government issued a decree authorizing the "militarization" of war industry, which involved placing the major industries under government control.[21] In agriculture, resistance was fiercer; the anarchists fought hard to preserve the peasants' collectives which they had established in the parts of the country under their control. On August 27, Uribe, the communist Minister for Agriculture, published a decree which, under the guise of promoting cooperatives and increasing grants to peasants, assured the peasant of complete freedom of choice between forms of cultivation – individual or collective. These provisions did not differ substantially from those already laid down in the decree of October 7, 1936. But in regions where anarchists had remained in power throughout the first year of the civil war, especially in Aragon, the collectives had held their own. Now that the central government had established its authority, many collectives were in fact broken up, and the land returned to individual peasant holdings, though how far this process had gone before republican rule itself ended, a year later, is uncertain.[22] A more surprising and little publicized concession was a decree of July 31 removing the ban on the performance of

---

between UGT and CNT see p. 31 above. Further negotiations between UGT and CNT in August were reported in *Rundschau*, No. 37, August 26, 1937, p. 1315.

[20] S. Payne, *The Spanish Revolution* (1970), pp. 309–310.

[21] M. Meshcheryakov, *Ispanskaya Respublika i Komintern* (1981), pp. 89–90.

[22] *Ibid.* pp. 88–89; a few months later Togliatti still complained that the "progressive policies" of the "Catalan comrades" had the effect of "pushing the peasants towards bourgeois and republican parties" (P. Togliatti, *Opere*, IV, i [1979], 306).

religious rites. Churches are said to have reopened in the republic for the first time on August 7.[23]

Of the problems confronting the PCE and its Soviet mentors in the autumn of 1937, the army loomed largest. Since the earliest days of the civil war, Comintern and the PCE had sought to unify the army by incorporating in it the militias and brigades initially recruited to stay the advance of the insurgents.[24] Prieto, the Minister of Defence in both Largo Caballero's and Negrín's governments, fully shared this purpose. So long as Largo Caballero was Prime Minister, his sympathy for the anarchists, who were the main opponents of integration, and his bad relations, personal and political, with Prieto, deprived the latter of any effective power.[25] But Negrín was a close political associate of Prieto in the PSOE, and a personal friend; and when he became Prime Minister, Prieto embarked on an active campaign to establish authority over the anarchist militias which manned the Aragon front.[26]

In August 1937 regular army units took over the Aragon front; and the Aragon provincial council, dominated by anarchists which had hitherto governed the region, was dissolved, doubtless not without reprisals against the leaders. Other military reforms

---

[23] M. Meshcheryakov, *Ispanskaya Respublika i Komintern* (1981), p. 127.

[24] See pp. 29–30 above.

[25] Togliatti in his report of August 30, 1937, took an unflattering view. The Spanish military forces were inefficient, ill-equipped and lacked discipline; they had no will to fight and were split by internal feuds. The communists and the international brigades were the best (P. Togliatti, *Opere*, IV, i [1979], 258–259).

[26] "Before the middle of 1937", according to the narrative of a Soviet military adviser, the long Aragon front was distinguished by a "remarkable calm". It was manned by Catalan units which were under the "strong influence of anarchist organizations", and had no stomach for "hostile clashes with the enemy"; fraternization across the line was a common phenomenon. *Pod Znamenem Ispanskoi Respubliki* (1965), pp. 173–174, contains reminiscences of Soviet participants. This account is motivated by malice at the expense of the anarchists; Orwell, who served on the Aragon front in the first months of 1937, confirms the calm prevailing at this time but not the fraternization (see G. Orwell, *Homage to Catalonia* [1938], *passim*). But it is clear that, before the advent of the Negrín government, little effort had been made to establish central control over the forces on the Aragon front, or to incorporate them in the "people's army".

were undertaken. The powers of the Supreme War Council and the general staff were increased. Military training at all levels was systematized. In September 1937 the people's army was said to have a strength of 575,000 men, divided into 152 brigades.[27] A success was achieved in combating illiteracy among the recruits; 70,000 soldiers were said to have been taught to read, and 6000 schools set up.[28]

The status of the international brigades raised special problems. By the summer of 1937, the initial enthusiasm which had generated the rush of foreign volunteers to defend the republican cause had fallen off; the French government had closed the French–Spanish frontier, and was discouraging the further flow of volunteers into Spain. The strength of the brigades could be maintained and increased only by the recruitment into them of Spaniards, including Spanish commanders and non-commissioned officers, a process rendered easy by the superior prestige and priority in supplies of food and weapons enjoyed by the brigades. Statistics of August 1937 revealed that of about 16,000 members of international brigades, 7171 were Spanish, 3158 French, 1186 Italian, 922 German, 772 Belgian, 686 British, 568 American, 449 Czech and Slovak, 396 Austrian and others.[29] These developments weakened any remaining claim to the autonomy or separate status of the brigades. On June 8 the chief of the general staff issued an order for their reorganization; and the structure and personnel of their base at Albacete were also modified. Then, on September 23, a governmental decree signed by Negrín provided for the final and complete integration of the international brigades into the people's army.[30]

While the PCE unreservedly applauded these measures, sharp clashes occurred over communist infiltration in the army. The

[27] M. Meshcheryakov, *Ispanskaya Respublika i Komintern* (1981), pp. 86–87.

[28] J. Hernández, *La Grande Trahison* (1953), p. 114.

[29] M. Meshcheryakov, *Ispanskaya Respublika i Komintern* (1981), pp. 109–110.

[30] *Ibid.* pp. 113–114; for the text of the decree see W. Rust, *Britons in Spain* (1939), pp. 200–205. According to a later report of Togliatti, trouble had been caused by delegates of foreign parties who attempted to intervene in the affairs of international brigades without consulting the PCE, and thus "fomented rivalry and nationalist strife within the brigades" (P. Togliatti, *Opere*, IV, i [1979], 302).

influence of the Soviet advisers increased constantly. Spanish officers of the people's army were sent to the USSR for training. According to PCE statistics, in the summer of 1937 60 per cent of all army personnel were party members, five out of eleven corps commanders, and 56 out of 72 brigade commanders. Of 1373 military commissars, 441 were party members, 260 members of the joint communist – socialist youth league, and 107 members of the PSUC.[31] Prieto was a firm believer in a professional army not involved in politics. He had no love for the PCE, or for the Left wing of the PSOE, which flirted with it; and he probably counted on Negrín's support in an attempt to curb the role of the communists in the army.[32] The PCE had offered provocation. Its central committee, at the session of June 18–21, 1937, decided to appoint representatives of party organizations in all military units, which would discuss all questions relating to the conduct of war, and ensure "the systematic carrying out by officers and commissars of the policy of the popular front".[33] Prieto retorted on June 27 with a decree "on the struggle against proselytism in the army", which prohibited all political work in the army.[34] Ibárruri attacked the decree in an emotional and uncompromising speech, which included the sinister reminder of the need not only to "organize the army", but also to "establish order in the rear".[35] In spite of hot-headed words, the increasingly dangerous military situation dictated a compromise; and in the sequel neither the party resolution nor Prieto's decree seems to have produced any significant change.

[31] M. Meshcheryakov, *Ispanskaya Respublika i Komintern* (1981), pp. 87, 92.

[32] This may have been a miscalculation; Prieto, long after in a letter of 1939, reproached Negrín with his failure to recognize the danger of communist domination in the army and the administration (D. Cattell, *Communism and the Spanish Civil War* [1965], p. 234, note 27).

[33] M. Meshcheryakov, *Ispanskaya Respublika i Komintern* (1981), p. 96; the text of the resolution has not been available and the remarks of Uribe, who presented it to the committee, were very briefly reported in the account of the session in *Kommunisticheskii Internatsional* (see p. 44, note 23, above). This reticence was probably prompted by the contentious and delicate turn which the question had taken.

[34] M. Meshcheryakov, *Ispanskaya Respublika i Komintern* (1981), p. 94. "Proselytism" meant the attempt of PCE organizations to induce army personnel, and especially new recruits, to join the party; the phrase in current use in Russian was "lovlya dush", and translated in English as "catching souls", was suggested by the biblical "fishers of men".

[35] D. Ibárruri, *Speeches and Articles* (1978), pp. 132–143.

Friction between Soviet advisers and their Spanish colleagues was one of the main preoccupations of Togliatti's sojourn in Valencia in the summer of 1937. His report of August 30 frankly placed part of the responsibility for unsatisfactory work of the PCE on "our advisers". His severest strictures fell on Codovilla, who had taken into his masterful hands all the tasks of the party central committee, turning himself into the "beast of burden". If Stepanov was placed in charge, Codovilla's methods could be changed.[36] Togliatti voiced these criticisms at meetings of the party politburo early in September, but met with opposition from Codovilla and from the German Dahlem, who was also present as a delegate of IKKI. After their departure (conceivably prompted by IKKI on Togliatti's initiative), things went better, and a document published by the party central committee on September 15 had its source in an article by Ibárruri written, according to Togliatti, "without any help or corrections on our part".[37]

The document made some concessions to the harsh realities of the military situation. It did not minimize the blows inflicted on the republic by the loss of Bilbao and Santander, by the failure at Brunete, and by Franco's blockade of the Mediterranean coast, though it continued to proclaim its faith in ultimate victory. But its positive injunctions had a well-worn air: unity of the anti-Fascist front, and the struggle against those who sought to sow dissent; unity of the PCE and the PSOE, and the removal of misunderstandings with the anarchist FAI and CNT. Communists in the army were exhorted to maintain strict discipline, and to "establish comradely and fraternal relations with commanders, members of other parties and organizations, with old officers who loyally and honourably serve the cause of the republican fatherland".[38]

Five days later, on September 29, 1937, IKKI adopted a resolution on the main tasks of the PCE. This placed strong emphasis on the democratic basis of the anti-Fascist front, and recommended common lists with other anti-Fascist parties at elections (a somewhat academic issue). National control of the

[36] P. Togliatti, *Opere*, IV, i (1971), 271–272; in his subsequent letter of September 15 (see note below), Togliatti named Uribe, Ibárruri, Hernández and Giorla as capable party leaders.

[37] *Ibid*. p. 272; see Note B, pp. 94–98 below.

[38] *Kommunisticheskii Internatsional*, No. 10–11 (1937), pp. 185–189; it appeared in *Frente Rojo*, September 15, 1937.

economy was essential for efficiency, involving agreement with the trades unions. Close relations should be sought with the national committee of the CNT; this should help to restore unity in the UGT, now challenged by the supporters of Largo Caballero. Only in the matter of fusion between the PCE and the PSOE was a restraining hand laid on the party's ardour. Nothing should be done to lend colour to the charge that the PCE wanted "to swallow up the socialist party".[39] It was probably also on this occasion that it was decided to withdraw Codovilla and Gerö from Spain, and entrust the Comintern representation there to the less aggressive Stepanov. Policy remained unchanged, but Soviet influence was to be exerted by milder, more self-effacing measures. Its hand could, however, hardly be concealed in an important *coup* executed on October 1, 1937, when the executive committee of the UGT removed Largo Caballero from the presidency of the organization, expelled several dissident federations, and declared its full support for the government.[40]

Military operations in the autumn of 1937 did nothing to encourage the republican cause. The much advertised July counter-offensive in Brunete had fizzled out. Franco's forces steadily mopped up the remaining republican strongholds in the north. The last of these, the port of Gijon, had fallen on June 22. Before the end of the year, the nationalists held the whole northern coast as far as the French frontier, the important mining and industrial Asturias region, and the greater part of Aragon, hitherto an anarchist base. Two-thirds of the territory of Spain was in the hands of the insurgents. The effective rule of the Spanish government was confined to Catalonia, to the Mediterranean coast as far south as Almería, and to a part of the central provinces, with Madrid precariously confronting a massive block of enemy territory. The last session of the Cortes in Madrid was held on October 1, when Ibárruri once more expounded the policy of the PCE and of the Catalan PSUC: efficiency in the army and in the defence industries, unity of all anti-Fascist forces, and an invitation to the CNT to join the government.[41] But Valencia also was now too exposed. The seat of government was transferred to Barcelona.

---

[39] The resolution does not appear to have been published; the fullest account of it available is in K. Shirinya, *Strategiya i Taktika Kominterna* (1979), pp. 168–169.

[40] M. Meshcheryakov, *Ispanskaya Respublika i Komintern* (1981), p. 124.

[41] D. Ibárruri, *Speeches and Articles* (1978), pp. 153–158.

The move of the government from Valencia to Barcelona in September 1937 may have been prompted primarily by military considerations. But it had the effect of strengthening the hold of the central government over Catalonia at the expense of the Generalitat, and curbing the ambitions of Catalan nationalists. A single authority replaced the uneasy dual partnership which had hitherto controlled the politics of a semi-autonomous province.[42] But the bogey of Catalan separatism could never be completely exorcized. The ánodyne formula adopted by the party congress of the PSUC in July 1937 revealed that Catalonia was, and was not, an integral part of Spain: "Catalonia cannot be free if Fascism conquers Spain. Spain cannot be made free without the help of Catalonia."[43] Togliatti went so far as to describe the move to Barcelona as to some extent a guarantee that Catalonia would not break the resistance front and conclude a separate peace, but admitted that it created difficulties attributable in part to neglect of Catalan susceptibilities. Though the PCE encouraged communists to join the PSUC, friction continued between the two parties. The PSUC was "under strong petty-bourgeois influence as it was under the influence of the anarchists and of POUM", and professed "ultra-Left" policies of collectivization and collectivism. But Togliatti admitted that the CNT was still the major force among the workers of Catalonia. It was not an encouraging picture.[44]

The meeting of the central committee of the PCE in Barcelona on November 13–16, 1937, was a routine affair. Díaz, in the main report, proclaimed the virtues of the popular front as "the greatest and broadest political organization that the Spanish people had ever had"; the country was "an anti-Fascist democracy of a new type". He called for new elections which would "still further mobilize the masses for the struggle against Fascism". This did not, however, imply that the PCE had forgotten that it was a proletarian party or had abandoned its own principles and political line. Ibárruri spoke on the need to strengthen the army. Uribe, the Minister for Agriculture in the government, attacked Largo Caballero for hypocritically pretending that the republic

[42] M. Meshcheryakov, *Ispanskaya Respublika i Komintern* (1981), p. 131, represents this, rather than the military situation, as the motive for the move.
[43] *Rundschau*, No. 24, May 4, 1938, p. 783.
[44] P. Togliatti, *Opere*, IV, i (1979), 303–308.

had abandoned the path of the revolution; and Hernández, the Minister for Public Education, eulogized "the achievements of the USSR over a period of twenty years, and the Stalin constitution". The committee exchanged cordial greetings with the PSOE, looking forward to the prospect of unification, but apparently took no further steps towards it.[45]

A report by Togliatti to Moscow ten days later gave a more realistic account of the underlying tensions. While assiduously avoiding any remark which might earn him the label of defeatist, and while firmly asserting that the government and public opinion was decisively against compromise, he confessed to the existence among "the masses" of a longing for peace, and for a withdrawal of Italian and German forces in return for territorial concessions. Unofficially, moods of compromise could be found in the PSOE (he did not mention the PCE). In Barcelona, defection was openly preached, though this could be attributed to Trotskyites, to sections of the anarchists, and to supporters of Largo Caballero. Togliatti did not fail to recall the bad influence of Codovilla and Marty in the PCE, and feared that this might still not have been wholly eradicated.[46]

Everything turned ultimately, however, on the military prospect; and control of the army was at the core of every conflict. Prieto, the Minister of Defence, though at one with the PCE in working for an integrated army under central control, constantly mistrusted the predominance of communists in leading posts. Here, he seems to have been foiled by the fact that communists provided the largest number of recruits, and often the best officers. But he enjoyed more success in his campaign against the military commissars – an institution in which communists had always played a principal role.[47] Unable to secure the abolition of the institution, Prieto starved its headquarters of necessary facilities, and vetoed the appointment of 300 new commissars. The ensuing compromise involved the resignation of Álvarez del

---

[45] *Kommunisticheskii Internatsional*, No. 12 (1937), pp. 54–57; Díaz's report and reply to the debate are in J. Díaz, *Tres Años de Lucha* (Paris, 1970), pp. 460–532.

[46] P. Togliatti, *Opere*, IV, i (1979), 280–287; later in a letter to Moscow of January 28, 1938, Togliatti spoke still more frankly of "defeatist moods", especially in Catalonia, where people talked of a "separate peace" with the enemy (*ibid*. 293–294).

[47] See p. 59 above.

Vayo, who had been at the head of the commissariat since its creation in October 1936; and thereafter its subordination to the Ministry of War was readily achieved. The PCE seems to have put up surprisingly little resistance to these measures.[48] Later, the military disasters of 1938 were attributed by Soviet sources to "the collapse and bureaucratization of the commissariat", the communists being replaced by "incompetent people who had no revolutionary firmness, faith or enthusiasm".[49] By May, 1938, 70 per cent of the posts were said to have been left unfilled.[50]

Nor were the signals from abroad encouraging. In Britain the annual Trades Union Congress and the Annual Labour Party Conference in the autumn of 1937 repeated with complacent approval their unimpressive performances in the Spanish question during the past year. At the Trades Union Congress, Citrine, in a wordy speech, introduced a resolution which deplored the denial to the republicans by the British and other governments of arms and equipment to meet the Fascist aggression, but relied for remedial action on the Council of the League of Nations. Nobody in the debate which followed had any fresh proposals to make.[51] The Labour Party Conference unanimously adopted a resolution condemning the so-called non-intervention agreement, and demanding the restitution to the constitutional Spanish government of its right to purchase arms in order to maintain its authority.[52]

In France, though the PCF was more vocal than the CPGB, effective support had also faded away. The fall of Gijon prompted a joint letter of the PCE and the PSOE addressed to the Second International and the Comintern, calling for a joint meeting of the two Internationals to consider the question of aid to the Spanish republic, on lines laid down at Annemasse.[53]

---

[48] M. Meshcheryakov, *Ispanskaya Respublika i Komintern* (1981), pp. 94–95; P. Togliatti, *Opere*, IV, i (1979), 285, alleges that Álvarez del Vayo played a double game, and had not broken with Largo Caballero. The bland narrative in Álvarez del Vayo's *Freedom's Battle* (1940), pp. 125–126, throws no light on what really happened; H. Thomas, *The Spanish Civil War* (3rd edn., 1977), p. 773, adds some embellishment to the story.

[49] *Bol'shevik*, No. 4 (1940), p. 32.

[50] M. Meshcheryakov, *Ispanskaya Respublika i Komintern* (1981), p. 135.

[51] *Trades Union Congress: Sixty-Ninth Annual Report* (1937), pp. 260–278.

[52] *Report of the Thirty-Seventh Annual Conference of the Labour Party* (1937), pp. 212–215.

[53] The letter, as quoted in J. Duclos, *Mémoires*, ii (1969), 243–245, is

Thorez and Cachin at once seized the occasion to address to de Brouckère and Adler a letter denouncing "the odious so-called policy of non-intervention – a one-way blockade – applied in violation of international law at the initiative of the governments of the democratic countries", and reiterating the appeal for an immediate meeting of representatives of the two Internationals. This drew the usual reply expressing sympathy in substance, but rejecting the proposed meeting.[54] A mass meeting in Paris in December, addressed amid scenes of enthusiasm by Ibárruri as well as by representatives of the three major parties of the French popular front, also offered nothing new.[55] That these demonstrations were regarded with some impatience in Moscow is suggested by a letter from Dimitrov to the PCE, of December 17, which insisted not only on the struggle against defeatists and compromisers, but on such practical tasks as the strengthening of reserves, and the improvement of supplies to the population.

---

undated; but the fact that the letter of Thorez and Cachin endorsing it is dated November 20, 1937, suggests that it was written after the meeting of the central committee of the PCE in November.

[54] *Ibid.* ii, 245–247.

[55] *Ibid.* ii, 224–228; an evidently unsuccessful attempt by the British TUC in December 1937 to mediate between officials and Caballerist wings of the UGT was recorded in *Trades Union Congress: Seventieth Annual Report* (1938), p. 173.

7

THE TASTE OF DEFEAT

It was perhaps the courage of despair which led the Spanish government in December 1937 to mount the largest republican offensive operation of the civil war against the provincial capital of Teruel, 200 miles east of Madrid, strategically a key-point on the road from Madrid to the Mediterranean coast, which had long been in Franco's hands. The city fell after some savage fighting in mid-December, and was held by the republicans until the end of February 1938. But its fall represented a temporary set-back for Franco, rather than a serious defeat. A manifesto of the PCE of February 24, 1938, attempted to minimize the significance of its evacuation by republican forces.[1] But its re-taking by Franco, after the exaggerated hopes engendered by its capture, was a bitter blow, and removed the last obstacle to Franco's break-through to the Mediterranean. By April 1938, 40 miles of the Mediterranean coast were in nationalist hands. Military defeat sparked off a governmental crisis. Togliatti reported to Moscow in January 1938 that relations with the PCE had improved, "a little through pressure, a little through persuasion", but that party–state relations were still "our weak point".[2] Friction between Prieto and the PCE had never been far beneath the surface; and Prieto was now openly branded in PCE circles as a defeatist.[3] In March the PCE sent to Negrín an elaborate set of proposals for the reform and reorganization of the army, which was obviously aimed at Prieto.[4]

The situation was now desperate. Early in March, Azaña, apparently prompted by the French ambassador in Barcelona,

---

[1] *Rundschau*, No. 10, March 3, 1938, pp. 311–312.

[2] P. Togliatti, *Opere*, IV, i (1979), 298.

[3] J. Hernández, *La Grande Trahison* (1953), p. 139, recalled an article by him in *Frente Rojo*, February 24, 1938, on the theme "Anyone who speaks of capitulation is a traitor", and a speech of Ibárruri in Barcelona on March 1 attacking Prieto as a "capitulationist".

[4] M. Meshcheryakov, *Ispanskaya Respublika i Komintern* (1981), p. 137; according to P. Togliatti, *Opere*, IV, i (1979), 314, no progress was made owing to obstruction by Azaña, the president.

called a special meeting of the government, to which he submitted proposals for peace overtures.[5] The parties of the Left reacted sharply. On March 14, 1938, the PCE issued a radio appeal to the Spanish people for aid from all anti-Fascists in achieving victory over Franco.[6] On the following day the central committee of the UGT and the anarchist CNT met and agreed on a programme of common action, which included wider powers of central economic controls;[7] and on March 15, a mass demonstration in Barcelona, said to have numbered 200,000, called on Negrín to continue resistance and to remove from the government ministers who were no longer willing to defend the republic, Prieto being the manifest target of attack.[8]

At this moment, however, events elsewhere in Europe impinged on the fortunes of the Spanish republic. On March 12, Hitler entered Vienna, and became uncontested master of central Europe, Mussolini being reduced to the role of subsidiary ally. For the Western democracies, whose concern with Spain had already waned in the autumn of 1937, it now became even more of a peripheral interest in meeting the threat presented by Hitler. In one of its now rather rare comments on the Spanish situation, *Pravda* connected the Fascist aggression in Spain with the conquest of Austria by "German Fascism" and with events in Czechoslovakia, and once more denounced the "two-faced" policy of the French and British governments.[9] At the end of March, the British and French governments seem to have suggested to Negrín that the time had come to look for a compromise settlement with Franco.[10] On the other hand, the need to overcome defeatist tendencies made it imperative to beware of the danger of weakening the popular or national front by any undue insistence on any kind of party doctrine. On March 29, Díaz addressed a letter of stern reproof to the party newspaper *Mundo Obrero*, which had published an article declaring that the struggle was between Fascism and communism, and that the

---

[5] P. Togliatti, *Opere*, IV, i (1979), 316; Togliatti also records, without dating it, a meeting of Azaña with leaders of the political parties, at which only Negrín and Díaz firmly resisted Azaña's defeatist line, and Díaz 'brutally" accused him of "abusing his powers" (*ibid.* 318).

[6] *Kommunistcheskii Internatsional*, No. 4 (1938), pp. 70–71.

[7] *Rundschau*, No. 16, March 17, 1938, p. 508.

[8] M. Meshcheryakov, *Ispanskaya Respublika i Komintern* (1981), p. 138.

[9] *Pravda*, March 31, 1938.

[10] *Dokumenty Vneshnei Politiki SSSR*, xxi (1977), 126–127.

enemy against which the republic was engaged in mortal combat was capitalism.[11]

What happened behind the scenes in the Spanish government crisis of April 1938 is not fully recorded. Prieto was relieved of his office as Minister for War and, having apparently refused any alternative portfolio, resigned from the government. Negrín himself became Minister for War. Members of the PSOE predominated. But an innovation was the inclusion of a representative of the UGT, who became Minister for Justice, and a representative of the CNT, who replaced the communist Hernández[12] as Minister for Public Education. But this loss of ministerial posts was balanced by the re-appointment as Minister of Foreign Affairs of Álvarez del Vayo who, though a socialist, was always reckoned as a strong supporter of Moscow. The central committee of the PCE set up a commission, significantly headed by Togliatti and Stepanov, to draft a programme for the new government. The draft was submitted to a representative meeting of party leaders, as well as the leaders of other popular front organizations. After "stormy debates" it was approved, and published in the party press on April 30 in the form of "thirteen points". It was designed primarily to maintain the independence and integrity of Spain. It promised the defence of democratic and civil rights, including the rights of property and the "free exercise of religious beliefs". A special clause, on which IKKI insisted and which caused some controversy, protected the property of foreigners, other than those who had helped the nationalists. Any element that could be labelled communist, or even socialist, was rigorously excluded. It was aptly remarked that the thirteen points represented the transition from the "popular" to the "national" front.[13]

Togliatti reporting at this time to Moscow gave a somewhat

---

[11] Díaz's letter was reprinted, with a note stressing its importance, in *Rundschau*, No. 24, May 4, 1938, pp. 751–752.

[12] Hernández's own explanation in *La Grande Trahison* (1953), p. 102, of his resignation is highly dubious; it does not accord with other accounts of his attitude at the time, or with his own account of his appointment at Mije's headquarters as commissar-general for a group of republican armies (*ibid.* p. 147). An interview with him in this new capacity was published in *Rundschau*, No. 25, May 5, 1938, pp. 830–831.

[13] M. Meshcheryakov, *Ispanskaya Respublika i Komintern* (1981), pp. 147–149.

contradictory view of the scene. The military situation was not good, and it was imperative to increase the supply of planes and arms. Negrín was in difficulties because he was accused of being a communist agent. The morale of the population was satisfactory, in spite of an "extremely grave situation in Barcelona"; the fifth column had been defeated, and there was no demoralization or disruption.[14]

The customary May 1 proclamation of IKKI for 1938 declared that "the Spanish republic is in danger", and repeated the empty appeal for united action with the Second and Amsterdam Internationals.[15] The party central committee meeting in Madrid on May 23–25, 1938, could take only a sober view of the prospects. The situation of the republic had "deteriorated considerably". The "most reactionary groups of the British and French bourgeoisie" were ready to "come to terms with the Fascist aggressor at the expense of Spain". Nevertheless, the party declared its undiminished faith, in conjunction with all other anti-Fascist forces, in "the will of the popular masses to make Spain an independent, free and happy country". The committee also sent a message of greeting and reassurance to Stalin.[16]

The move of the capital to Barcelona symbolized the growing, and indeed almost exclusive, importance of Catalonia in republican strategy. As the area under the control of the republic gradually contracted, and Franco's advance operations cut off Catalonia from the remaining territory held by the republic, it became the one base from which any effective resistance could still be organized. But this made the situation of the communists in Catalonia, and of the communist-dominated PSUC, more delicate than ever. At a session of the central committee of the PSUC in June 1938, after Comorera, the general secretary, had insisted on the need for joint action by the PCE and PSUC to counter "manoeuvres" to separate Catalonia from the rest of Spain and break the united anti-Fascist front, Ibárruri delivered another impressive appeal. She recalled that the PCE and the PSUC had, from the first, been committed to the defence of "the democratic parliamentary republic", and rejected the view of

[14] P. Togliatti, *Opere*, IV, i (1979), 323–324.
[15] *Rundschau*, No. 23, April 28, 1938, p. 708.
[16] For an account of the proceedings, and the text of the telegram to Stalin, see *Rundschau*, No. 30, June 2, 1938, pp. 993–995; for the text of the resolution see *ibid*. No. 31, June 9, 1938, pp. 1023–1025.

some comrades who mistrusted the government programme of the thirteen points. The strength of the CNT should not be underestimated, and concessions might have to be made to the need for "proletarian united action". All "sectarianism" must be avoided. So comprehensive an appeal suggested a large measure of desperation.[17]

The reconstitution of the government in April 1938, which was a conscious attempt to overcome the defeatist moods engendered by the failure at Teruel and Franco's advance to the coast, enjoyed a larger measure of success than might have been expected. On July 26, 1938, Ibárruri spoke at another open-air demonstration in Paris, destined to be the last exercise of the kind. Passionate assurances of republican victory, and cries of "Open the frontiers", seemed to belong to an earlier stage of the war, but were still heard with enthusiasm.[18] Humbert-Droz, at the same moment, briefly revisiting Barcelona, depicted an extraordinarily optimistic atmosphere prevailing, at any rate in communist circles. Barcelona was like Moscow in the period of the civil war. The people showed admirable qualities of endurance and courage. The victories on the Ebro would "upset Chamberlain's plans built on the defeat of the republic".[19] Early in August, Togliatti left on a visit to Moscow, and did not return to Spain until the middle of September. In Moscow it was a grim moment. The last of the public purge trials had ended with the execution of Bukharin and Rykov in March 1938. But the reign of terror, culminating in the execution or exile to Siberia of large numbers of army officers, officials, suspected dissidents and members of foreign parties, was at its height. Togliatti may be presumed to have discussed the Spanish crisis. But his only recorded activities in Moscow related to the Polish, Italian and Swiss parties.[20]

[17] *Rundschau*, No. 35, July 7, 1938, p. 1166.

[18] *Humanité*, July 29, 1938; D. Ibárruri, *Speeches and Articles* (1978), pp. 253–263. The French version is slightly longer, but the two tally closely.

[19] J. Humbert-Droz, *Dix Ans de Lutte Antifasciste* (Neuchâtel, 1972), p. 336; for the campaign on the Ebro, see below.

[20] P. Togliatti, *Opere*, IV, i (1979), cxvi–cxviii. The presence of Togliatti was required at the session of IKKI at which the decision to disband the KPP was announced. This seems a unique case of a wholesale liquidation of a "fraternal" party and the physical extermination of its leaders. In 1961 Togliatti described the decision (in *Rinascita*, December 1961) as mistaken and catastrophic. The party was rehabilitated in 1956 (*Trybuna Ludu*, February 19, 1956).

Though Franco's advance now seemed inexorable, republican resistance was not yet quite exhausted. The last heroic republican offensive of the war was an advance of the people's army at the end of July 1938, from the north across the river Ebro, where for two or three months it successfully over-ran positions not very firmly held by Franco's troops. The "battle of the Ebro", celebrated as a republican victory, disorganized and impeded Franco's projects for a final assault on Madrid. But more than this it did not achieve; the operation seems, like the battle for Teruel, to have been more costly to the attackers than to the defenders, and the disparity between the forces at the disposal of the combatants was increasingly apparent. In November, Negrín wrote a despairing letter to Stalin begging for an increase in military aid from the USSR.[21] No answer is on record. Madrid and Barcelona went hungry, though there was still plenty of food in the countryside.

Moreover, by the time the battle of the Ebro petered out, in November, the international situation had been dramatically transformed. When the battle was launched in August, it was still possible to speak, though no longer very plausibly, of the concerted Western and Soviet reaction to the threat of the Fascist dictators. The Munich agreement of September exploded this illusion. By way of corollary it was clear that a Franco victory in Spain would cause no more than the mildest ripple on international waters. When the agony of the Spanish republic entered its final stages, the eyes of Europe were fixed elsewhere. The intangible repercussions of the Munich agreement throughout Europe affected Spanish republicans in two ways. They showed more clearly than ever that Spain had now been relegated to an insignificant place in the preoccupations of the European powers, and also that no future efforts to sustain the democratic cause in Spain could be expected from those who had so easily abandoned it elsewhere. Díaz, on October 5, 1938, wrote in the journal *Frente Rojo*: "What occurred in Czechoslovakia is a defeat for the international proletariat, a defeat for the forces of democracy and peace. Fascism has won a victory."[22]

Nor did the repercussions in the European parties of the Left bring any aid or comfort to the Spanish republicans. According to a report by Togliatti, the parties of the Second International

[21] *Guerra y Revolución en España*, iv (Moscow, 1977), 198–200.

[22] J. Díaz, *Tres Años de Lucha* (Paris, 1970), p. 367.

were bringing covert pressure to bear on the Spanish government and on the PSOE to come to terms with Franco. The British Trades Union Congress already in September 1938 made much of its generous contributions to an international solidarity fund providing relief to the suffering Spanish people. But an appeal from the UGT for political support received short shrift. It was the eve of Munich, and other international issues dominated the scene, leaving little attention for the death-throes of the Spanish republic.[23] Largo Caballero visited the Labour party leaders in London, and Zyromski of the SFIO visited the leaders of the PSOE in Spain. Adler also came to Spain in December for conversations with Negrín. The result of all these journeyings was to sour relations between the PSOE and the PCE, and to represent the PCE as the enemies of peace.[24] Besteiro, the old and long-discredited leader of the Right wing of the PSOE, emerged from retirement to propose the formation of a government acceptable to France and Britain; by implication this would have been a government which excluded communists and sought an accommodation with Franco.[25]

The reconstruction of the Negrín government in April 1938, and the "thirteen points" of April 30, had marked the final abandonment of any revolutionary element in the republican programme, and identified the republican cause with the defence of the national independence and integrity of Spain against Fascist assailants who relied primarily on foreign aid. It was part of the same process which had transformed the original international brigades into predominantly Spanish units integrated into the national army.[26] A resolution of the secretariat of IKKI of September 3, 1938, urged the PCE to work for national unity, and to wage a "decisive struggle" against defeatism. But it also issued a warning against the "syndicalization" of industry, and "administrative pressure" on the peasantry. It gave its blessing to the reopening of churches in Madrid, Barcelona and Valencia,

---

[23] *Trades Union Congress: Seventieth Annual Report* (1938), pp. 175–180, 367–371.

[24] These points were made in a report by Togliatti dated May 21, 1939 (P. Togliatti, *Opere*, IV, i [1979], 346); see Note B, pp. 100–101 below. The report was written in Moscow; a typed text in French, with Togliatti's handwritten corrections, remained in his archives.

[25] *Ibid.* IV, i, 352; for Besteiro, see p. 1 above.

[26] See pp. 29–30 above.

and to "the maintenance of the closest unity with the Catholic and other peoples of Spain".[27] The Assembly of the League of Nations at Geneva in September 1938 (the last of a series which had begun full of hope in 1920), meeting at the height of the Munich crisis, had little thought to spare for Spanish affairs. But Negrín, in his speech on September 21, scored a point by proposing the withdrawal of all foreign volunteers from Spain, to be supervised, in place of the manifestly impotent non-intervention committee in London, by the League of Nations. It is unlikely that this move impressed the Italian or German authorities. But the Negrín government now set to work seriously to repatriate the volunteers serving in the international brigades. A farewell parade, addressed by the irrepressible Ibárruri, was held in Barcelona on November 15, and some 10,000 volunteers left for their respective countries under the watchful eye of a League of Nations commissioner.[28] The great international campaign against Fascism, so eagerly inaugurated in Spain in 1936, had been wound up, or transformed to a broader, worldwide context.

In Spain the battle of the Ebro delayed Franco's victory by some weeks. But when the republican effort collapsed, the way into Catalonia was open to Franco's forces. The advance began on December 23. The enemy closed in on the capital; and a rallying cry from the PCE beginning "Catalonians! Spaniards! The fatherland is in danger" was no more effective than a joint appeal of the UGT and the CNT to all workers in Europe and America, or a particularly emotional manifesto, presumably drafted in Moscow, but issued in the name of the communist parties of the principal European countries, as well as of the United States and Canada, addressed among others to "Catholics, Protestants, Jews, believers and non-believers who love peace".[29] Thorez, at the national conference of the PCF on January 21, 1939, enumerated the many vital issues which separated the party from the Daladier government, but exclaimed:

---

[27] *Georgii Dimitrov: Vydayushchiisya Deyatel' Kommunisticheskogo Dvizheniya* (1972), pp. 352–353.

[28] H. Thomas, *The Spanish Civil War* (3rd edn, 1977), pp. 851–853.

[29] These documents appeared in *Rundschau*, No. 3, January 19, 1939, p. 77; No. 4, January 26, 1939, pp. 107–108; the joint appeal of the communist parties was also published in *Humanité*, January 27, 1939, and in *Kommunisticheskii Internatsional*, No. 1 (1939), pp. 87–89.

The decisive question at this moment for France is to save Spain! Open the frontier! Help Spain. Our reservations on your general policy remain. But if you open the frontiers, we are ready to support you.[30]

On January 26, 1939, the first nationalist tanks rolled into Barcelona. The indiscriminate massacre of republicans went on for some days. The population, war-weary and hungry, accepted the inevitable. The remnants of the battered republican army crossed the frontier into France, preceded and followed by a horde of refugees; it stands to the credit of France that these were at least not turned back. Declarations by Negrín and Álvarez del Vayo, of a determination to fight on even after the fall of Barcelona,[31] were as empty as other gestures of this tragic moment. *Pravda* blamed "the criminal non-intervention policy operated by the governments of the bourgeois-democratic countries, France and Britain" for the tragedy of Catalonia, and praised those communists who continued the struggle in Madrid and in the towns and villages of the central zone.[32]

The whole of Spain was now in Franco's hands, except for a roughly triangular wedge whose apex was Madrid, and base the Mediterranean coast line from Valencia to Almería. Togliatti, with a handful of members of the PCE and of the government, including Negrín, established themselves for a few days at Figueras in the north of Catalonia. Here, in an atmosphere of total confusion, the Cortes on February 1, 1939, held their last session, attended by 62 members out of the over 450 elected three years earlier. Negrín, speaking in the name of the government, recognized the situation as hopeless, and proposed an offer of peace negotiations on three conditions: a guarantee of the independence of the country, the right of the Spanish people to decide on its governmental system, and the cessation of victimization and interrogation of those who had taken part in the war. The proposal was approved by Mije in the name of the PCE,[33] and unanimously adopted. On February 9, groups of government

---

[30] *Oeuvres de Maurice Thorez*, XVI, iv (Paris, 1956), 162–3.

[31] *Rundschau*, No. 5, February 2, 1939, p. 137.

[32] *Pravda*, February 7, 1939.

[33] M. Meshcheryakov, *Ispanskaya Respublika i Komintern* (1981), pp. 182–184; P. Togliatti, *Opere*, IV, i (1979), cxxii (the introduction to the volume,

and party leaders crossed into France and found a momentary resting place in Toulouse. Here a general dispersal took place. Azaña, with some of his closest associates, refused to continue the struggle and, still the President, retired to the residence in the Spanish Embassy in Paris. Negrín and Álvarez del Vayo flew back in a French plane to Alicante, still in republican hands, ostensibly in order to organize a last desperate stand against the Fascists. Togliatti, accompanied by some members of the PCE, re-entered Spain at Tolosa, south of San Sebastian, and after a dramatic night flight reached Madrid on February 16. He found that Negrín had arrived there before him, and had embarked on discussions with Casado, the commander of the garrison, who was convinced that further resistance was hopeless, and was by this time looking for a negotiated surrender.[34]

Charges and counter-charges by supporters of Negrín and Casado make it difficult to disentangle exactly what happened in Madrid in the later part of February 1939. Casado by this time made no attempt to conceal his detestation of communists;[35] and Togliatti and his companions from the PCE played no part in these proceedings. The censorship banned publication of the PCE resolution of January 28, presumably on the ground that it attacked the government for its failure to rally its forces after the fall of Barcelona. The PCE defied the ban and circulated the document, and this led to recriminations with the PSOE and an open breach of the popular front. The communists were branded as the only party which was not in favour of peace, and enjoyed little sympathy or support. Negrín avoided contact even with

---

written by Spriano), 374–376. Mije's declaration was said to be based on a decision of the party central committee of January 28, which was subsequently criticized by Togliatti as unrealistic (*ibid*. IV, i, 384–385); but it is not surprising that a dispersed and distracted central committee should have spoken at this time with different voices.

[34] S. Casado, *The Last Days of Madrid* (1939), pp. 105–106, dates Negrín's arrival as February 28, and his four-hour conversation with Negrín as taking place on the following day; but this is inconsistent with other dates in this hastily compiled and confused volume, and is manifestly wrong. P. Togliatti, *Opere*, IV, i (1979), cxxiv, gives February 12 as the date of Negrín's arrival in Madrid.

[35] It was widely believed that the presence of communist ministers in the republican government was the cause of the hostility shown to it by the French and British governments; when Largo Caballero visited London in December 1938, Attlee and Morrison tried to disabuse him of this idea, but without success (P. Togliatti, *Opere*, IV, i [1979], 346).

Uribe, the communist minister in his government.[36] The politburo of the PCE in Madrid attempted to retrieve its position
by a manifesto of February 22 which claimed that peace did not
mean surrender, but could be achieved on the basis of the three
conditions of the government statement in the Cortes on February 1.
This, according to Togliatti, made "a great impression".[37]

But relations also quickly soured between Casado and Negrín,
who ruled out the possibility of negotiation with Franco. A
meeting of the government on March 1 showed that most of its
members wanted to negotiate, and Negrín tried in vain to stem
the polemics against the communists.[38] A few days later, Negrín
and his ministers, now in a state bordering on despair, left
Madrid and settled in the small town of Elda, a few miles inland
from Alicante, destined to be the last resting-place of the
republican government in Spain. Casado's patience was now
exhausted by Negrín's hesitations and reservations; and on the
night of March 5–6, in a radio address, he announced the
formation of a Council of National Defence, which included
General Miaja, the veteran Right-wing socialist Besteiro, and
representatives of the CNT and UGT, and promised the people of
Madrid and the army "a well-deserved and honourable peace".[39]
It was a fruitless exercise. Communist units, knowing too well the
fate which awaited them in the event of surrender, refused
Casado's call to lay down their arms, and fought fiercely to the
last. Franco turned a deaf ear to any suggestion of negotiations,
and would be content with nothing short of total and uncon-
ditional surrender. But Casado's defiance marked the effective
demise of the Negrín government. A telephone conversation
between Elda and Madrid ended in a declaration of war between
the two men. Negrín formally dismissed Casado from his
command. Casado formally repudiated an authority which in
fact no longer existed.[40]

---

[36] This picture emerges from Togliatti's report of May 21, 1939 (P. Togliatti,
Opere, IV, i [1979], 385–386).

[37] *Ibid.* IV, i, 387.

[38] M. Meshcheryakov, *Ispanskaya Respublika i Komintern* (1981), pp. 187–
188.

[39] S. Casado, *The Last Days of Madrid* (1939), p. 151.

[40] Several accounts of this conversation were current. According to the most
picturesque of these (in H. Thomas, *The Spanish Civil War* [3rd edn, 1977],
p. 903), Casado announced that he had staged a revolt. "Against whom?" asked

About the same time Togliatti and his companions of the PCE, after another adventurous flight, also left Madrid and reached Elda. Here on March 6, at a site not far removed from government headquarters, a depleted and dispirited politburo decided that it was time for the central committee to leave the country. The exodus of Soviet advisers took place without publicity, and must, by this time, have been almost complete. Ibárruri and other party leaders made for Paris. The affairs of the party on the spot were left in the hands of Togliatti and Checa, a member of the party central committee who had played a prominent part in recent developments.[41] Togliatti's plans, however, whatever they were, were interrupted by a dramatic episode.[42] On the night of March 6–7, Togliatti, with Checa and another member of the PCE, Claudin, set out from Elda for the coast-town of Murcia, where a communist organization existed. On the way they were arrested by a military patrol loyal to Casado and hostile to the communists, who took them first to Alicante, and then to Albacete, both believed to have gone over to Casado.[43] At Albacete, however they found some still loyal communist forces, together with a Russian military commission headed by someone masquerading under the name Martínez. These helpers succeeded in extricating Togliatti and his companions from the hands of their captors, and hid them in a house in the city where they remained till March 10. On that day they made their escape, and apparently went to Valencia, since on March 11 Togliatti and Checa met Hernández and other comrades "in the mountains near Valencia".

Negrín. "Against you," replied Casado. A shattered Negrín gave up the unequal struggle, and departed for Toulouse. Togliatti called it "a tragic mistake and quite inexplicable" (P. Togliatti, *Opere*, IV, i [1979], 337).

[41] M. Meshcheryakov, *Ispanskaya Respublika i Komintern* (1981), p. 189.

[42] Three apparently authentic accounts of this affair (Spriano's introduction in P. Togliatti, *Opere*, IV, i [1979], cxxv; Togliatti's letter to Ibárruri and other members of the PCE of March 12, 1939 (*ibid.* IV, i, 325–327); and his final report of May 21, 1939 (*ibid.* IV, i, 398–399)) exhibit some inconsistencies of detail and dating; see Note B, pp. 100–101 below.

[43] The revolt of Casado against Negrín resulted in what Claudin later described as a "small civil war within the great civil war". The military patrol which arrested Togliatti and his companions acted on the orders of P. Sayagües, head of SIM in Alicante, who was to deliver them into the hands of the Casado junta in Madrid, where they would have almost certainly been imprisoned or even executed. As a Republican and a friend of Claudin from their student

It was while they were in hiding in Albacete that Togliatti and Checa drafted a document, which was issued in the name of the central committee of the PCE, bearing the date March 10, 1939, and calling for an end to resistance, whether to the nationalists or to Casado's national council. It admitted frankly that the masses had turned away from the PCE because the masses wanted peace. It was essential to regain the confidence of those who disapproved of the Casado junta, and to re-establish the popular front. The aim was to prevent any further useless sacrifice of communist lives, and to build for an unknown future.[44] The tortuous argument was characteristic of Togliatti's pen; and he was, beyond doubt, the main author of the manifesto.[45] He is also said to have sent an emissary to Madrid with instructions to the communist forces still in the city to end the now useless struggle. He followed this up on March 12 with an exceedingly confused letter to Ibárruri and other comrades in Paris. The letter began with a realistic assessment of the impotence and complete isolation of the PCE; Negrín was under suspicion of collusion with Casado. Togliatti insisted on the importance of the retention by the PCE of its legal status – presumably a warning against rash and provocative action. But it ended with some highly fanciful speculations on the possibility of the Casado junta reforming itself

---

days, he felt he could not do this with a clear conscience. Instead, he sent the arrested men to Albacete under the escort of a trusted officer, on the tacit understanding that he would turn a blind eye to any attempt to escape on the way (Claudin's letter to T. Deutscher of March 6, 1983).

[44] *Guerra y Revolución en España*, iv (Moscow, 1977), 323; M. Meshcheryakov, *Ispanskaya Respublika i Komintern* (1981), p. 191.

[45] Nobody afterwards cared to claim responsibility for the manifesto, which seemed to smack of defeatism; and direct attribution of it to Togliatti comes from hostile and unreliable sources. Spriano coyly remarked that Togliatti and Checa issued an appeal on March 10, "to gain a few days' time" and rally friends of the party against Casado (P. Togliatti, *Opere*, IV, i [1979], lxxiv–lxxv). Several passages in Togliatti's letter to the Spanish comrades of March 12 (see Note B, pp. 98–100 below) read like an apologia for the manifesto of March 10; the PCE was completely isolated, and could not take responsibility for bringing the war to an end "in circumstances of such bloody chaos as can scarcely be ignored". Togliatti's authorship of the document is confirmed by Claudin. He remembered that while at Albacete, Togliatti was "very calm, despite the great risks he was running. He wrote a document in which he still tried – in a very Italian manner – to arrive at a compromise with the junta of Casado, to re-establish the unity of the republic. But it was too late" (Claudin's letter to T. Deutscher, March 6, 1983).

and ending its persecution of communists, of a reconstruction by the PCE of the popular front, and even of the fall of Franco and the succession of a government willing to negotiate conditions of peace.[46] Finally, Togliatti asked that the letter, when read, should be sent "home" (presumably to Moscow). Togliatti also telegraphed an urgent request to the Soviet government, through the Soviet Embassy in Paris, to send ships to take off a maximum number of refugees – a request to which, for practical reasons, a response can scarcely have been expected.[47]

What happened in the next ten days to the group of PCE leaders congregated in Valencia and other towns of the coastal region remains obscure: evidence is confined almost entirely to the report written by Togliatti after his safe return to Moscow.[48] Togliatti's ultimate aims, once the situation was recognized as hopeless, were to secure the evacuation of as many of the communist leaders and fighting forces as was possible, to save what was left of the PCE from extermination, and to lay the foundation of an underground organization to function under the predictably Fascist future regime. His immediate impulse was to stir up opposition to Casado among other military leaders and in the PSOE. The only document of the period is a manifesto of the central committee of the PCE of March 18, 1939. It refuted the standard accusations that the PCE wanted to attack the republic, and that it was a "foreign" party. The PCE wanted peace; Negrín's three conditions of February 1 were recalled. The real culprits were those socialists and anarchists who had acted in collusion with Casado. The manifesto made a passionate appeal to the socialist workers and members of the UGT, and to the council, workers and members of the CNT, "not to allow the curse to fall on them of Cain who killed his brother". It ended with a salute to the independence of Spain, to the popular front, and to the PCE as the vanguard of the working class and of the Spanish people.[49]

[46] P. Togliatti, *Opere*, IV, i (1979), 325–332; the draft in Spanish, written by hand with corrections, is in Togliatti's archives; it was, presumably, typed and sent, though there is no actual evidence of this.

[47] P. Spriano, *Storia del Partito Comunista Italiano*, iii (1970), 272–273.

[48] This report was marked "Strictly Confidential" and dated May 21, 1939 (P. Togliatti, *Opere*, IV, i [1979], 343–410); see Note B, pp. 100–101 below.

[49] *Rundschau*, No. 24, April 13, 1939, pp. 621–623, where it is described as emanating from the central committee of the PCE in Madrid; but its

These efforts achieved no positive results. A policy of resisting Casado, once resistance to Franco had been abandoned as hopeless, appealed neither to rival generals nor to socialists and anarchists; and nothing occurred to modify the general hostility now excited by the communists. An attempt to expel communists from the UGT was narrowly averted. The rank and file of the PCE, on Togliatti's testimony, "did not in the last period acquit itself well". The leaders realized that nothing was left to them but to save their own skins. A new party centre, presumably to direct underground work, was set up in Valencia. Togliatti and a select band of leaders – Togliatti names Hernández, Checa and Uribe – arrived on March 21 at Cartagena, which, after the Casado *coup* earlier in the month, was believed to have returned to communist allegiance. This, unfortunately, proved untrue. But at length, on March 24, Togliatti and his party were able to force an entry to the air-force camp and commandeer three aeroplanes. In these they took off and, flying without instruments, landed at Mostaganem in French North Africa. Togliatti, now equipped with a Chilean passport, took ship at Oran for Marseilles, crossed France to Le Havre, and there embarked on a Soviet ship on which Ibárruri and other Spanish communists from Paris also travelled. They arrived in Leningrad some time in May.[50]

If the instruction of March 10, 1939, to end the fighting ever reached the communists in Madrid, it was not obeyed. Communist military units fought desperately to the last, and delayed the final surrender of the city till March 29. It was followed by a predictable reign of terror. The coastal towns surrendered without resistance a few days later. Casado's revolt against Negrín's derelict government earned him no gratitude from Franco. He and a few hundred out of an army of refugees escaped to safety on a British naval vessel. On April 1, the United States recognized Franco's government, leaving the USSR as the only major power which had failed to do so.

But the last days of the Spanish republic were masked from the eyes of the world by the imminence of other dramatic events.

---

appearance in P. Togliatti, *Opere*, IV, i (1979), 333–342, from a Russian text with numerous corrections in Togliatti's hand (*ibid.* IV, i, 251–252), seems conclusive proof of Togliatti's authorship.

[50] Togliatti's report is supplemented by details in Spriano's introduction (*ibid.* IV, i, cxxiv–cxxvi), and M. Meshcheryakov, *Ispanskaya Respublika i Komintern* (1981), p. 191.

Stalin, in his major speech to the eighteenth Soviet party congress on March 10, 1939, mentioned Spain in passing only as one of the targets of German and Italian territorial ambitions.[51] Manuilsky, who reported next day on the work of Comintern, consoled his hearers with the comforting reflexion that the "miracle" of the long resistance of republican Spain to an overwhelming superiority of military force had been due to the united front of the working class, fortified by "the great political strength of the growing communist party", and "above all" to the political support of the Soviet Union and of the father of all workers, comrade Stalin. But he also dismissed "the Munich bargain" as being, among other things, "a conspiracy against the Spanish republic"; the loss of Catalonia was "a direct consequence of Munich". Towards the end of his speech he praised the heroism of the PCE, and named Díaz and Ibárurri as "steadfast Stalinists, of whom the whole international communist movement is proud".[52] But nobody contemplated the magnitude of the disaster, or considered any possibility of remedial action.

Before the congress ended, Czechoslovakia had altogether displaced Spain as a central focus of the international scene. On March 15, 1939, Hitler marched into Prague. April 1 was the date of the Anglo–Polish treaty guarantee; and from that moment, the danger of war was never far from men's thoughts. Nobody is likely to have been impressed when the PCE and PSUC in exile issued a May 1 manifesto proclaiming their faith in the independence of Spain and "the re-conquest of the democratic republic".[53] The British Labour party held no conference in 1938, having decided to transfer the date of its annual conference from the autumn to Whitsuntide. When it met at the end of May 1939, all was over in Spain, and the calamity of the Spanish republic was overshadowed by the looming threat of a European war. A resolution of the conference declared, in the face of all evidence, that "the cause of Spain is not lost", held the British government responsible for "the martyrdom of the Spanish people", and exhorted it to make all possible provision to aid Spanish refugees. It was carried without a vote after a brief but acrimonious debate

---

[51] Stalin, *Sochineniya*, xiv (Stanford, 1967), 334.

[52] *XVIII S"ezd Vsesoyuznoi Kommunisticheskoi Partii (b)* (1939), pp. 53–55, 60.

[53] *Rundschau*, No. 27, May 4, 1939, pp. 711–712.

provoked by a handful of delegates who sought to condemn the past ineffectiveness of party action. But few consciences were seriously ruffled in the process.[54]

From this time Spain was no longer a political issue, and raised only humanitarian questions of aid to refugees. At the end of January, the secretariat of IKKI had already proposed a non-political international committee of public figures to deal with the question.[55] An international committee was formed in Paris to relieve the misery and scandal of the French internment camps in which Spanish refugees were herded; the total number is said to have reached 325,000. An international conference was held in Paris on July 15–16, 1939, heralded by a well-publicized appeal by Hernández, who quoted Manuilsky's tribute to those who had fought in defence of the republic, and urged that the refugees should be released from the concentration camps and organized as a force of resistance to Fascism throughout the world. The 421 participants in the conference, drawn from 34 countries, included de Brouckère, who had just retired from the presidency of the Second International, Cot and Marty; and messages of sympathy were received from Negrín, from the Mexican government, and from Norman Angell. The conference passed a resolution appealing to "the consciences of all men and all free peoples" on behalf of the refugees and of members of the international brigades who could not return to their own countries; and informal quotas were drawn up of numbers which each country might be asked to receive.[56] Gradually the refugees were dispersed throughout the world, the Spanish-speaking countries of Latin America receiving the largest contingents. By August 1 Mexico had received 6500 refugees.[57] About 8000 are said to have settled in the USSR.[58]

In Moscow, the rump of the central committee of the PCE in July 1939 recalled the third anniversary of the outbreak of the civil war and of the glorious days of resistance to Franco and his

[54] *Report of the Thirty-Eighth Annual Conference of the Labour Party* (1939), pp. 250–264.

[55] M. Meshcheryakov, *Ispanskaya Respublika i Komintern* (1981), p. 193.

[56] *Rundschau*, No. 39, July 20, 1939, pp. 1126–1128; *Kommunisticheskii Internatsional*, No. 7 (1939), pp. 53–55; for Hernández's appeal, see *Rundschau*, No. 37, July 6, 1939, pp. 1037–1039.

[57] *Ibid.* No. 41, August 3, 1939, p. 1188.

[58] M. Meshcheryakov, *Ispanskaya Respublika i Komintern* (1981), p. 194.

Fascist allies.[59] In December, Díaz and Ibárurri both contributed articles to an issue of the Comintern journal, celebrating Stalin's sixtieth birthday.[60] But these were pious memories of a now distant past. With the outbreak of the world war the problem of Spain acquired an entirely new political dimension.

The significance of the Spanish civil war in the history of Comintern is that it provided a strikingly dramatic testing-ground for the doctrine of the "united front", which had slowly gained ground in Comintern in the early nineteen-thirties and had been formally adopted, amid scenes of enthusiasm, at its seventh congress in 1935. In Spain, even before the outbreak of the civil war a year later, the prospects of a united front between communists and socialists were more promising than elsewhere, partly because the communist PCE had never been strong enough to present a serious challenge to the socialist PSOE, but mainly because of the prominence of a powerfully supported anarchist workers' movement which was a rival to both. The civil war, which made resistance to Franco a paramount need, not only promoted the united front between PSOE and PCE, but paved the way for partially successful attempts to draw the anarchists into the fold. So far, the original concept of a united front of workers held good. But soon, as in France, and here far more acutely, the question arose of relations with radicals of the Left who, while opposed to socialism, were prepared to cooperate in current politics with socialists and even communists on an "Anti-Fascist" platform. For communists, this implied a collaboration with bourgeois democracy which had already been foreseen and approved at the seventh congress. The "united front" of workers was transformed into the "popular front".

But the logic of events carried the transformation a step further. In France, Thorez liked to strike a note of patriotic fervour, and to depict the PCF as the party which loved its country and cherished its traditions. In Spain, the massive Italian and German forces supporting Franco's military campaigns made it easy to identify resistance to Franco with the defence of Spain's national independence and the integrity of her territory. In the later stages of the war, though phrases like "democratic republic" continued in use, the supporters of the Spanish government were

[59] *Kommunisticheskiĭ Internatsional*, No. 7 (1939), p. 40.
[60] *Ibid*. No. 11–12 (1939), p. 66.

those who, irrespective of political opinions, were ready to fight to save Spain from Franco and his foreign auxiliaries. As a Soviet official historian wrote, "Spain was the first country in western Europe where the democratic dictatorship of a broad coalition of political forces, from communists to Catholics, based on parliament, was established."[61] The "popular front" became a "national front".

These successive transformations, however, though they occurred almost as a matter of course, did much to confirm the apprehensions of those purists in Comintern who had feared the dilution of communist doctrine inherent in the advocacy of the united front. The false dawn of revolution in central and western Europe after 1919 faded. The confident belief in Moscow, that the Russian revolution was the first stage in a European or world revolution, proved illusory. Yet it remained enshrined, ideologically, in the party creed and, institutionally, in the worldwide organization of Comintern, and could not be lightly abandoned. Stalin discounted it from the first. By the nineteen-thirties he regarded it as a positive nuisance and as an obstacle to a prudent policy designed to protect the interests of the USSR. In the early nineteen-thirties Stalin was preoccupied with the colossal problems of collectivization, and resistance to his own leadership in the party. It is unlikely that foreign affairs attracted much of his attention. But Hitler's seizure of power, and Dimitrov's dramatic performances, brought the issue back into the limelight, and in the course of 1934 Stalin encouraged Litvinov's attempt to secure rapprochement with the western powers, and moved towards support for Dimitrov's policy of the "united front against fascism and war". From the end of 1934 he patiently assumed this line, ably seconded by Dimitrov, and it became official policy at the Seventh Congress of Comintern. In the year which separated that Congress from the Spanish civil war, opposition to the new line was gradually worn down and crushed. Long before the war in Spain reached its final stages, any ideological element that smacked of socialism or communism had been sedulously eliminated from the programme of the government ardently supported by the PCE and Comintern; the programme indeed contained points directly opposed to communist doctrine. Nor was play any longer made with the

[61] *Istoriya Vtoroi Mirovoi Voiny,* ii (1974), 51.

theoretical argument that support for bourgeois democracy was a first stage on the road that led to a socialist revolution. The issue was one of pure expediency. The more desperate the situation became, the more evident it was that everything must be done, and everything sacrificed, in order to strengthen flagging resistance to Franco. The issue of the subordination of Comintern to the interests of Soviet foreign policy was ever present in Spain. But in the end, both Comintern and the Soviet government were concerned to prevent Franco's victory, yet neither had at their disposal adequate means to achieve this purpose.

In one significant respect Comintern and Soviet policy in Spain represented a landmark. Guidance from Comintern to foreign communist parties had been familiar from its earliest years, and had increased in intensity as time went on. But never before had a party so small and obscure as the PCE before 1936 been so rapidly promoted to a predominant role in the affairs of the state. It was notorious that this occurred not through any outstanding participation of communists in the tasks of government (there were never more than two subordinate communist ministers, and "La Pasionaria" was the only member of the PCE to achieve any kind of eminence), but through the constant and active direction of Comintern delegates of several different nationalities, and by Soviet advisers attached to every important branch of the administration; and the acceptability of these was a product of Spanish dependence on military and other supplies, equipment and technical aid which it received from the USSR. All this, in the later stages of the war, seemed to have less and less to do with communism; and in this sense it represented a subordination of communist principles to considerations of a policy which merely used communists to achieve its ends. It was a system which found wider application in eastern Europe after the liquidation of Comintern and the end of the Second World War.

[NOTE A[1]]
EXCHANGE OF LETTERS BETWEEN STALIN AND LARGO CABALLERO

To Comrade Caballero

Our representative plenipotentiary, Comrade Rozenberg, has transmitted to us the expression of your fraternal feelings. He also told us about your unwavering faith in victory. May we express our fraternal thanks for your sentiments and assure you that we share your faith in the victory of the Spanish people.

We consider and shall always consider it our duty to come, within our possibilities, to the aid of the Spanish government which is leading the struggle of all toilers, of the whole Spanish democracy, against the Fascist-military clique, the agency of international Fascist forces.

The Spanish revolution is following a path in many respects different from that which Russia had followed. This is due to different social, historical and geographical conditions, and to the different international situation which Russia had to face. It is quite possible that in Spain the parliamentary way will prove more appropriate towards the revolutionary development than was the case in Russia.

We still think, however, that our experience, especially that of our civil war, may have a certain importance for Spain if one bears in mind the specificity of the conditions of the Spanish revolutionary struggle. This is why we have agreed, responding to your repeated demands transmitted to us at various times by Comrade Rozenberg, to put at your disposal a number of military instructors. Their task will be to advise and help in military matters those Spanish military leaders to whom they are assigned.

It has been categorically impressed on them that they must always remember that, notwithstanding the full awareness of solidarity which at the present time binds together the Spanish people and the peoples of the USSR, a Soviet comrade, being a foreigner in Spain, can be truly helpful only on condition that he adheres strictly to the role of an adviser, and an adviser only. We think that this is precisely the manner in which you will make use of our military comrades.

As friends, we would ask you to inform us how effectively our military comrades fulfil the task you entrust them with; it is obvious that only if you judge their work positively would it be useful for them to continue.

We would also ask you to let us know, openly and frankly, your opinion about Comrade Rozenberg: is the Spanish government satisfied with him or should he be replaced by another representative?

And here are four pieces of friendly advice for your consideration:

1. One should pay attention to the peasantry, which, in such an agrarian

---

[1] *Guerra y Revolución en España*, ii, (Moscow, 1971), 96–97.

country as Spain, is of great importance. It would be advisable to issue decrees relative to agrarian problems and to taxation which would be favourable to the peasantry. It would also be advisable to attract the peasants to the army or to organize partisan peasant detachments at the rear of the Fascist armies. This would be facilitated by decrees furthering the interests of the peasantry.

2. The petty and middle urban bourgeoisie should be attracted to the government side and be given at least the chance to occupy a neutral position, which would favour the government, by protecting it from attempts at confiscation and securing as far as possible the freedom of trade. Otherwise these strata will follow the Fascists.

3. The leaders of the Republican party should not be repulsed, but on the contrary, should be drawn in, brought nearer and associated with the common exercise of government. It is especially important that the government should secure the support of Azaña and his group and that everything should be done to help them in overcoming their vacillation. This is necessary in order to prevent the enemies of Spain from regarding it as a communist republic and to forestall their intervention, which would constitute the greatest danger to the republic of Spain.

4. It would be advisable to find an opportunity to state in the press that the Spanish government will not condone any action against the property rights and the legitimate interests of those foreigners in Spain who are citizens of states which do not support the rebels.

Fraternal greetings
Friends of Republican Spain
Stalin, Molotov, Voroshilov

December 21, 1936

Letter from Largo Caballero to Stalin, Molotov and Voroshilov

Dear Comrades,

The letter which you were so good to send me through Comrade Rozenberg gave me a great deal of pleasure. Your fraternal greetings and your fervent faith in the victory of the Spanish people gave me profound satisfaction. I wish, on my part, to respond to your heartfelt greetings and to your fervent faith in our triumph by sending you the expression of my warmest sentiments.

The help you are providing to the Spanish people, and which you yourselves – considering it as your duty – have undertaken to provide, has been and continues to be greatly beneficial. You may rest assured that we rightly appreciate it. From the bottom of my heart, and in the name of Spain, and especially on behalf of the workers, we assure you of our gratitude. We trust that, as in the present, so also in the future your help and advice will continue to be available to us.

You are right in remarking that there are substantial differences between the developments which followed the Russian revolution and those which follow ours. In fact, as you yourselves note, the circumstances in which the two revolutions occurred differ: the historical conditions of each people, the geographical position, the economic situation, the social and cultural development and, above all, the degree of political and trade union maturity are not the same. But, in answer to your other remark, one should perhaps state that, whatever may be the future of the parliamentary form, it does not possess among us, or even among the republicans, enthusiastic defenders.

Those comrades who, responding to our call, came to our aid, are rendering us great services. Their vast experience is useful to us and contributes notably to the defence of Spain in her fight against Fascism. I can assure you that they are bringing to their task genuine enthusiasm and extraordinary courage. As to Comrade Rozenberg, I can say in all sincerity that we are satisfied with his behaviour and activity. He is liked by everybody here. He works hard, so hard that this affects his already undermined health.

I am very grateful to you for your friendly advice contained in the latter part of your letter. I regard it as a proof of your friendship and your concern with the successful outcome of our struggle.

The agrarian problem in Spain is, indeed, of exceptional importance. From the first, our government took it upon itself to protect the peasants by improving their living conditions enormously. Towards this end, important decrees were announced. Unfortunately, certain excesses in the countryside could not be avoided, but we earnestly hope that they will not be repeated.

The same should be stated concerning the petty bourgeoisie, which we have respected by constantly proclaiming its right to exist and develop. By defending it against the attacks to which it might have been exposed at the beginning, we are trying to attract it to our side.

I completely agree with what you say about the republican political forces. We have, in all circumstances, associated them with the tasks of the government and with the struggle. They participate largely in all political and administrative bodies, local, provincial and national. What happens, however, is that they themselves do practically nothing to define their own political individuality. As to the property of foreigners established in Spain who are citizens of countries which do not help the rebels, their rights have been respected and interests safeguarded. That has been stated on several occasions, and we shall continue this policy. I shall certainly re-state this worldwide at the first opportunity which presents itself.

Fraternal greetings,
Francisco L. Caballero.

Valencia, January 12, 1937

[NOTE B¹]

EXCERPTS FROM PALMIRO TOGLIATTI'S CONFIDENTIAL REPORTS TO THE HEADQUARTERS OF THE COMMUNIST INTERNATIONAL, MOSCOW

Report of July 8, 1937²

During the discussions with the LSI [Second International] representatives, I have endeavoured to send you direct information almost every day, either by telephone or in the cables transmitted back by our delegation. I shall continue to utilize these means of communication to keep you informed about the development of the discussions, which will resume tomorrow evening, 9 July, between de Brouckère on one side and Thorez and Cachin on the other. I am taking advantage of the opportunity that has presented itself today to send you a few impressions of a general character on the most urgent questions.

(a) First of all, Annemasse and relations with the LSI. The result of the Annemasse meeting was a surprise, especially for our French friends who, influenced by the fairly tense situation that prevails in their party's relations with the SFIO undoubtedly took for granted a completely negative response from de Brouckère and Adler. The protocol of the Annemasse meeting undoubtedly represents a step forward in our struggle for international unity of action; but I want to warn you against any excessively optimistic interpretation. It is worth underlining that what was achieved at Annemasse was achieved without any great effort on the part of our delegation.

De Brouckère and Adler arrived at Annemasse with a communiqué they had already drafted, refused any new formulation that might signify a precise commitment to concrete joint action, and accepted only a few minor improvements in the form of the text they had drawn up in advance.

But they were very friendly to our comrades, spoke openly of their disagreement with the English, the Dutch, etc., spoke openly about their resignations, saying that these had been provoked by a difference of opinions concerning the problem of united action, and also added that the joint communiqué must be

---

¹ These extracts, taken from Togliatti's *Opere*, vol. IV (1979), are reproduced here by kind permission of the publishers, Editori Riuniti, and the Editor, Professor Paolo Spriano. The translation is by Quintin Hoare. (Omitted passages are marked by ellipses.)

² This report was in fact written just before Togliatti's arrival in Spain and deals with the meeting of the representatives of the Second and Third Internationals in Annemasse which took place on June 21, 1937. See pp. 48–49 above.

drafted in very moderate terms so as not to allow the "others", "their successors", to ruin everything. I think this attitude means that de Brouckère and Adler had no intention of abandoning their positions as president and secretary.

By coming to Annemasse and signing the joint communiqué they wished, first and foremost, to give satisfaction to the Spaniards and prevent the Spanish Socialist Party from moving away from the LSI; but at the same time they were preparing the ground for the compromise that was reached at the Paris meeting. At the Paris meeting it seems (information given us by Delvigne) that de Brouckère caused a great stir behind the scenes, even saying that he was ready to leave for Moscow "to meet Stalin" and continue the struggle for unity; but he did not take any decisive action. The great majority was against him (all except the French, they told me). Cordero,* representing the Spanish party, was like-wise unable to struggle to defend his party's positions favouring international unity of action. But on the other hand the English, Dutch, and other rightists showed they were well aware how impossible it was for them, in the existing situation, to dispense with de Brouckère and Adler: that would have meant the LSI becoming totally discredited in the eyes of the masses, and perhaps before long a split in the LSI. This is why they accepted the compromise: they did not disavow Annemasse, but they undoubtedly laid down as a condition that de Brouckère should take no further steps towards an understanding and joint action with us.

So Annemasse was: 1. a result of pressure from the masses, and first and foremost of the pressure exerted on figures like de Brouckère by the Spanish working-class organizations; 2. an episode in the internal crisis through which the LSI is passing.

Annemasse does not as yet mean that the positions of the reactionary elements in the LSI, the enemies of the united front, have been greatly weakened.

Consequently, it will not now be easy to take new steps forward in the direction of a genuine and effective joint action. There is a danger that the modest positive result achieved may be nullified by a reaction from the rightists. Future advances can be the result only of continuous, tenacious activity carried out systematically and intelligently: a mode of action which clings onto the little that has been achieved, and avoids giving any pretext to the reactionary elements who will do everything possible to reduce that little to nothing. In this, we must rely much more than we have hitherto upon the independent work of our parties. This is the main conclusion to be drawn from all that has happened so far. And I stress this conclusion, because I am afraid that the meetings, Annemasse, the joint communiqué, etc. have created a different conviction within our parties. I am afraid there has been created within our parties a state of mind of more or less confident *expectation* regarding the development of our discussions with the LSI, etc. This state of mind is dangerous. The new con-versations will undoubtedly give us something, but nothing decisive as yet, and the stronger the pressure from below the more they will give us.…

---

* Manuel Cordero, member of the executive committee of the PSOE (the socialist party led by Francisco Largo Caballero, Prime Minister September 1936–May 1937, and Indalecio Prieto). [*Footnote from the Italian text*]

Report of August 30, 1937[3]

...The [Spanish] party has changed radically. It has become a large party, which undoubtedly contains the best part of the people in its ranks. It is filled with combative spirit, enthusiasm and initiative. Its authority has grown in an extraordinary fashion. Its leaders expound in a highly popular form all that the people understand, wish and feel. Therefore, they are popular and loved by the people. Our party is at present the only organization in Spain with a mass character and its own revolutionary programme for victory in the war, and that strives to implement such a programme. At the decisive moment in November at Madrid, and on decisive questions (the peasant question, the army), our party proposed the implementation of a specific political line and course of action to save the situation. But despite these positive aspects of the party, and our consciousness of its historic role in the war and the revolution, we must not shut our eyes to the defects that still survive in its work, so that we may remove them in time. Such defects are linked to the difficulty of the situation, the rapid growth of the party and the weakness of its cadres, for the most part young and inexperienced.

The party has understood one thing very well: that it must wage a coherent struggle to extend and reinforce its positions in the army, police, state apparatus, etc. Reinforcement of the party's positions in the army, first and foremost, and in the state apparatus is one of the main guarantees of victory. In my opinion this battle must continue. We must not lose any of the positions we have already won, wherever we have to conquer new ones. If the party should be criticized for anything, it is for its inability to utilize the fall of Largo Caballero's government to capture important new positions.

The party has not as yet learnt to develop a political activity capable of breaking the enemy's forces by implementing a coherent popular front policy. In this field, it seems to me it is necessary to carry out a whole number of adjustments to the party's policy.

The success achieved in the overthrow of Largo Caballero's government has undoubtedly gone to the heads of some comrades. They have decided that the success was due solely to the party, forgetting that Prieto* and the centrists had played a very important role in both the preparation and the solution of the crisis. This false assessment contributed to the view coming to the fore that now the party can pose the question of its *hegemony*, and struggle openly for this hegemony in the government and in the country. When the difficulties with the new government began, they thought the only way to overcome them was by creating a government with communist participation. When the anti-communist bloc began to form, though their starting-point was the correct observation that the struggle against the communists is a result of their growth, they slipped into the "theory" that considers it inevitable and foredoomed that all the non-communist parties one after another should line up against us. It is

---

[3] This report was written in Russian, addressed to "The Secretariat of Comrade Manuilski. For Com. Dimitrov from Ercoli" and signed "Alfredo". (Here translated from Italian.)

* Indalecio Prieto y Tuero, leader of the right in the socialist party, was Minister of Defence in the Negrín government until April 1938. [*Footnote from the Italian text*]

enough to speak with our comrades and listen to their debates to become aware that, even today, they still have not achieved adequate clarity on the question. One of the tasks awaiting us is to explain it to them and help them to understand it. In Catalonia, this confusion reached the point where the comrades had defined their main task as being to "struggle for the destruction of all capitalist elements" and to "check the strengthening and revival of the capitalist elements", thus arriving at the logical conclusion that such a policy could be carried out only by a proletarian and communist government. I send you a copy of a pamphlet – an open letter to the UGT – in which this theory is formulated. It is clear that, from this angle, the confused comrades could not grasp the fact that after the fall of Caballero their task was, on the one hand, to exert pressure on the government to secure the implementation of a popular front policy and, on the other, to prepare an enlargement of the government's basis, by stimulating through appropriate political work a differentiation in the ranks of the anarchists and Caballerists. Now and in the coming period, this is the only political course that can carry us to victory. In implementing this line, the party has undoubtedly experienced a few oscillations in the most recent period.

On the question of fusion with the socialist party, we have now succeeded in recovering a little of the time lost. The preparatory work for the fusion is adequate. But the resistance from the socialist leadership – I am speaking of the centrists; the Caballerists as you know are virulently opposed to it – is still very strong. Surprises are possible. We must skilfully continue the work of persuading the centrist leaders using coordinated pressure from below, making a mighty effort to protect the party from a split and avoiding any unexpected actions. So far as the Caballerist group is concerned, it is clear that they will not enter a united party: it will be necessary to make sure that they are isolated.

So far as the question of the anarchists is concerned, in my view we have not merely oscillated, we have indeed committed real errors also on tactical questions. The party as a whole is not correctly oriented on this question....

...After the overthrow of Caballero, the party did not understand the need to draw the anarchists closer to ourselves and to prevent any rapprochement between them and the Caballerists. We dithered. At the beginning of July the negotiations started, then suddenly for no obvious reasons.... The letter that explained why the negotiations were broken off and the communists moved away has disappeared from the party archives, while the anarchists are forever quoting passages from this letter to show that we communists do not want to work together with them. But still graver errors were committed, in my opinion, in relation to the drawing up of the UGT–CNT pact. The fact is the party opposed the pact, thus ensuring that Caballero would emerge as the champion of trade union unity at this juncture, and that the anarchist press would publish whole pages of resolutions on unity, while we are portrayed as enemies of the latter. The party did not understand that the pact, drawn up against us, could have been used against its proponents if we had monopolized the movement for a rapprochement between the two union federations.

Now the comrades understand the need for a rapprochement with the anarchists, and state that they intend to accomplish this; but at the same time they emphasize that this is no easy matter, both because it means imposing a real change of direction on the party forces, and because among the anarchist leaders there are many real scum closely linked to Caballero, most bitter enemies of the party and the popular front. Only through a vast activity from below will it be possible to isolate and paralyse all attempts at violent action against the government.

Closely linked with the question of the anarchists is the problem of trade union work.

I shall write about this after a more careful study of the question. What is already obvious is that this is the weakest factor in the party's work. At the moment this is one of those questions around which all difficulties accumulate. The trade unions have won great economic power, and this must be taken into account. The difficulties we have encountered in giving effect to the slogan of nationalization are due mainly to the unions. I request you to formulate the question in the following terms: is it possible to find an intermediate slogan and intermediate organizational forms, which will not immediately remove control of industry from the unions, but which could allow entry of the State organs into the running of industry and preparations for nationalization? I put this question to you because putting the nationalization slogan into effect means, in fact, expropriating the trade unions of those riches conceded to them by the revolution that they consider as their own. In some cases the workers agree, and it will be possible with the government's help to carry out this nationalization with their support. In other cases it will not be possible for us to put it into practice immediately, and we shall therefore temporarily have to agree to certain concessions. In Spain, the unions have their traditions and history, and these must be taken into account.

The popular front. Only with activity on the party's part is it possible to secure an improvement in this field. This means: it is necessary to revive the activity of the popular front committees where these already exist and to create new ones, etc. But this will not lead to a decisive improvement. On this question too, I should like you to examine with the comrades the possibility of assuming responsibility for a democratic initiative thanks to which it might be possible to impel the broadest possible masses into action, to mobilize them in an organized manner to sustain the government, and to implement a military policy. I am not thinking of the possibility of elections – Cortes or municipal elections – since this is not possible given the political situation, and since they would end up in shooting. But it would be possible to find watchwords related to the popular front committees capable of activating the masses. One might advise the president of the republic to launch, together with the leaders of the other parties, an appeal for the creation of a patriotic and mass organization to organize resistance to the enemy...that would take on the task of raising the morale of the masses on the home front and enlarging the basis of support for the government, promising the latter the backing of all decent Spaniards....

...It is necessary to demand of the comrades a radical improvement in the work of the centre, and to help them in this. The help you can give consists in sending comrades (instructors) to expand the central party school and strengthen the new cadres.

I do not wish to conceal from you my impression that responsibility for the centre's bad work falls partly upon our "advisers". In particular, it is necessary to persuade L.* of the need for a radical change in his own methods of work. The

---

* Louis, pseudonym of Vittorio Codovilla, an Argentine communist of Italian origin

Spanish comrades are grown up, it is necessary to understand this and let them walk on their own two feet, really limiting ourselves to the role of "advisers". It is essential to demand that L. stop being the beast of burden of the entire CC, that he transfer the operational work to the Spanish comrades and give up being the person without whom nobody does anything or knows how to act. This would give the Spanish comrades a sense of greater responsibility, and would greatly help them to work better. In the second place: the role that L. now fills prevents him from approaching things critically, whereas it is precisely in this that the essence of the role of an "adviser" from IKKI consists. It is thus inevitable that he should be criticized. In the third place: demand of L. that, in accordance with the rule, all meetings with members of the Spanish government, ministers, party leaders, etc. should be held by Spanish comrades. It is unacceptable that Caballero should have known of the party's decision on the question of fusion with the socialists from comrade Ch., then from L. and only a month later from Pepe Díaz! So far as Moreno* is concerned, I have nothing to say apart from the fact that he must have confidence in L., so that the latter may become convinced of the need to change his own methods of work. In connection with the perspective of fusion with the socialists, the question of the need for a change in L.'s work methods must be resolved as swiftly as possible.

with warm greetings

Alfredo, 30.8.'37

P.S.   It is clear that, on the question of my own work, I urge you to leave me here as long as possible, if only to study the evolution of the situation.

To Comrades D. and M.†

September 15, 1937

Dear comrades,
   A few words just to explain to you what has been done so far, following your advice and directives.
   Today a statement from the politburo is appearing throughout the party press, which is intended by the politburo itself to constitute the first step towards correcting the party's tactics on various points.

---

and founder-member of the Argentine Communist Party, which he represented on the Executive Committee of the Comintern after its Fifth Congress. [*Footnote from the Italian text*]

   * Ch. is Pedro Checa, member of the CC of the PCE in charge of organization, who had represented his party at the Annemasse meeting. Pepe was the nickname of José Díaz Ramos, Secretary of the PCE. Moreno was a code name for "Stepanov", in reality the Bulgarian communist Stepan Minev, in charge of the Comintern secretariat for Latin Europe between the Sixth and Seventh Congresses and dispatched to advise the PCE during the Spanish Civil War. [*Footnote from the Italian text*]

   † Georgi Dimitrov and Dimitry Manuilsky, the two most senior members of the Comintern's political secretariat. [*Footnote from the Italian text*]

The document was drafted after Louis' departure. I shall explain to you later why we were unable to begin before. The first *open* critical observations were made – by your friend Alfredo – in the politburo meeting that preceded the departure of C. and F.* Unfortunately, however, they had no practical outcome during this meeting. I would add that I was pretty dissatisfied with F.'s intervention and the position he took up in this meeting. In fact after the discussion was turning – with Checa's report and the interventions by Hernández and above all Uribe† – towards the correct direction of self-criticism and the search for what must be done to improve the party's tactics and work, F.'s intervention, by raising a whole series of so-called practical problems regarding the government's activity in the most diverse fields, completely disoriented the comrades and obscured the basic problem: the necessity for the party to pursue the popular front policy coherently. After F.'s departure, the conversations and discussions continued in the secretariat and the politburo and I am very pleased with how things went.

Precisely in the course of these discussions and conversations, the conviction grew in me that a radical change is necessary in the way your "advisers" operate in our situation here. Quite apart from Díaz, absent as you know through force of circumstance, and from Checa, there exists a group of comrades (Uribe, Dolores, Hernández, Giorla)‡ capable of leading the party and indeed leading it well. It is necessary, however:

1. That your "advisers" do not disorient these comrades by pushing them onto an erroneous path, either through the manufacture of improvised, incorrect theories, or through an inappropriate political excitability which, in combination with the Spanish comrades' own, ends up by gradually derailing the party's tactics; this criticism relates to F. and also to Pedro.§

2. That your "advisers" leave off considering themselves the "*bosses*" of the party, in the belief that the Spanish comrades are worthless; that they leave off substituting themselves for the latter, on the pretext of doing things "quickly" or "better", etc. This criticism relates to F. in particular. If the latter cannot change his methods of work, it is necessary that he not come back. Each day that passes strengthens this conviction within me.

The document published today genuinely constitutes the product of the entire Politburo's collective work. Once they have taken the path of a critical examina-

---

* Doubtless Codovilla and Franz Dahlem, a member of the CC of the German Communist Party, representative of the IKKI in Spain and a member of the political commission in charge of the International Brigades after December 1936. [*Footnote from the Italian text*]

† Jesús Hernández Tomás, member of the political bureau of the PCE, formerly in charge of propaganda and editor of the communist organ *Mundo Obrero*, was minister of education in the Caballero and Negrín governments; after April 1937 he was overall political commissar for the central zone. Vicente Uribe, member of the political bureau of the PCE, was minister of agriculture in the Caballero and Negrín governments. [*Footnote from the Italian text*]

‡ Luis Giorla, member of the political bureau of the PCE. [*Footnote from the Italian text*]

§ Pedro was Ernö Gerö, the Hungarian communist who had formerly represented the Comintern in the French party. Sent to Spain around April 1936, he worked with the Catalan Communist Party. [*Footnote from the Italian text*]

tion of the party's activity, the members of the Politburo show that they possess quite remarkable maturity and capacity of judgement, and themselves take the initiative in drawing the consequences of the critical observations made collectively. The Politburo document was preceded by an article from Dolores (written by Dolores on her own initiative, without any help or correction on our part), very good and which has already caused a bit of a stir; and by two articles from Giorla which have likewise occasioned surprise at their altered tone, and to which one of the anarchist dailies responded this morning in a pretty friendly way. However, I consider all this, and the document itself, simply as the first step needed to clear the air of the electric charge accumulated in the course of whole months of fierce polemics. The real political work will begin when the negotiations with the anarchists of the CNT get under way, in a few days time. The difficulties will be considerable, since it is a question of carrying through the rapprochement with the CNT without breaking or cooling relations with the socialists and the other parties in the PF [popular front]. This outcome can be achieved with a bit of skill....

...Each point in the document would require a comment to explain what in fact should specifically be corrected. But I do not have the time now to do this; moreover, I am not sure whether matters are clear to you after the discussions with Checa and with F. I want only to emphasize that, in my view, the party's activity must undergo a *double* correction: on the one hand, in the direction of consistently putting the popular front policy into practice (the Politburo document is the first step in *this* direction); on the other, in the direction of giving ever greater importance within the party's overall policy to the defence of the immediate interests and the aspirations of the working class, rural labourers and poor peasants – naturally within the framework of the popular front policy. The question of work within the unions, where we are still lagging far behind and things are not going well, is not raised here. I have been here for more than a month, and never once has a trade union question been discussed by the secretariat. Yet there are undoubtedly a whole number of burning questions of a trade union character, concerning workers' wages, etc., from which the party cannot remain aloof. In the party press there is no regular trade union coverage nor are there reports from the factories, which confirms that trade union work is still being neglected and that our links with the mass of factory workers are weak. What mainly interests the comrades is the political tendency struggle within the unions (winning leadership positions, etc.); but in this struggle they are still oriented more towards agreements at the top than towards mobilization of the masses organized in the unions on the basis of defence of their interests. This is one of the reasons why Caballero retains very important positions inside the unions and his union cadres remain virtually intact. Let us take the case of Valencia. The Caballerists control the regional leadership of the unions in this city, which means that they have at their disposal a daily newspaper, the *Correspondencia de Valencia*, organ of the Valencia trade unions. Today, this paper is Caballero's organ, and wages the filthiest battles against the c.p. [communist party]. The question has been before the secretariat since I arrived, and every day the comrades pledge that they will evict the Caballerists from the regional union leadership and the editorial board of the newspaper. Their plan consists in reaching an agreement with the socialists (centrists) present in the regional leadership and then, since together they would have a majority, carrying out a kind of semi-legal coup against the paper, throwing out the Caballerist editors and installing a new editorial board. They guarantee that the matter can be accomplished with the authorities' help, and promise daily that it will all be accomplished in 24 hours. For my part, I urge them and push them energetically in this direction. Finally, seeing that no progress whatsoever is being made, I entreat the comrades to study the problem thoroughly and discuss the question anew in the secretariat. Outcome of this discussion: the authorities have never promised to help us take over the paper; the rules and customs of the working-class movement do not permit an intervention of such a kind; the only possible intervention (after a decision by the judges!) would be by the Minister of Labour, who is an enemy of the party and would not agree; and the centrist socialists would not agree to a coup; and finally, if we wish to continue along this road, the only thing to do is to launch an attack on the paper with the party's own men and weapons – with the risk of having the police against us and the certainty that such an act would solidify the ranks of the Caballerist faction, make it more difficult for us to isolate Caballero, and worsen our relations with the anar., the government and also with a part of the working-class masses. In this way a month has been lost in discussion with the socialists, with the authorities, etc., etc., and during this time there has been total neglect of the most elementary mass work: mobilization of the workers in the plants and union assemblies against the paper and its editors; dispatch of protests, delegations, collective resolutions, etc. etc. In other words, in my view the essential thing has been neglected, thus allowing Caballero to organize his offensive against us . . . .

. . . One question that has been preoccupying us in the past few days has been the discipline of the communist cadres in the army (the best ones, unfortunately). Here too, ugly and *very dangerous* situation. I leave the details to one side. The fundamental point is that the communist cadres in the army do not feel the CC's authority. Whence there derives an impermissible struggle among them that undermines discipline, self-control, etc. We are intervening with a letter signed by the CC to the communist cadres in the army, and with other appropriate measures.

All the observations that I am making to you reflect also the opinion of Moreno, whom, I repeat, I blame for one thing alone: for not having done anything up till now to guide the comrades towards a correct self-criticism, to avoid very grave errors, etc. It is likewise with Moreno's agreement that I have asked you not to send Louis back. I did not wish to deliver any hasty judgement on his work, but now I think I may conclude that *his presence is harmful to the party*. Reasons: (a) he is the main person responsible for the fact that the p. [party] over these past few months has not carried out a consistent policy of popular front, rapprochement with the anarchists and isolation of Caballero: the way in which he posed the main problems could only disorient the party; (b) personally I consider him the main person responsible for the light-minded way in which party polemics have been conducted in the press (and partly at meetings too), delivering blows right and left without any plan, in such a way as to make impossible any logical and coherent development of political action, aimed at isolating open enemies and consolidating the popular front; (c) because his presence prevents the CC from working well, by destroying in comrades any sense of responsibility, critical spirit, etc.

I think that by the time you receive this letter you will already have taken a

decision on the matter, but given the seriousness of the problem I am keen that
you should nevertheless know my opinion. It is my opinion that we have made a
most serious error in leaving the Sp. p. [Spanish party] in such a situation, under
L.'s tutelage.

my warmest greetings
Er.

Report of March 12, 1939[4]

Valencia
Sunday, March 12, 1939

Dear friends,

As today is the first day of relative calm since our separation, and the possibility has come up of a comrade's departure for France, I am preparing these
brief sheets to inform you as precisely as possible about our situation and the
general situation in the country. I believe you are already aware of the fact that,
shortly after your departure from the airfield, the latter was surrounded by
Assault and SIM [Military Intelligence Service] units which, without daring to
launch an attack ("to avoid bloodshed" we were told by the Alicante SIM
commander, who reasonably enough stood in some awe of our guerrillas), had
watched the three planes take off. Unfortunately, these units arrested us as we
were attempting to get onto the road to Murcia without passing through the
checkpoints, and shut us up in the town-hall at Monovar. In the morning they
took us to Alicante under arrest, and there throughout the day our situation was
very uncertain, the alternatives being a long period of detention, release, or a
*paseo.** It seems that during the preceding twenty-four hours a number of
comrades from Alicante and other detainees had been *paseados.* The party
offices were under occupation by the police. Finally we succeeded in convincing
the SIM commander (a socialist) to free us and take us to Albacete under his
protection. Our car, weapons, driver, escort and guerrilla fighters: all lost. At
Albacete we succeeded in contacting Valcárcel, who secured a room for us in the
house of an unknown comrade; but Valcárcel himself and this comrade were
arrested just as they were leaving the house where we lay, and so far they have
not reappeared. We found ourselves once again without a contact, and with no
possibility of moving around or working, given that the situation at Albacete was
at least as confused and difficult as that in Alicante, since the order had gone
out to arrest all leaders of the party and all communist commanders or commissars, and it was impossible to pass through the roadblocks or circulate on the

---

[4] This letter, of three pages, addressed to Comrade Dolores and other members of the
Politburo, is handwritten in Spanish and signed "Alfredo".

* Refers to the "walk" taken by someone to be executed without trial. [*Footnote from
the Italian text*]

streets without special documents issued by the "new" authorities. A comrade from the airforce got us out of trouble by loading us into his car and taking us to a village near San Clemente, in Cuenca province; but the next day he abandoned us to our fate, which obliged us to set off on foot in search of a new way out of our plight. In the end we made contact with Alonso, Mendiola, Ananios and Camacho and saw some airforce comrades; but these gentlemen, though they had every conceivable means at their disposal and enjoyed almost normal relations with the Casado junta,* refused us any assistance at all, even the means to run off a PB statement which we had already prepared, and right down to items of clothing that we requested, to allow us to circulate more easily on the streets. Alonso, after promising us cars and documents to cross over into the Valencia zone, sent a message that *we could go there on foot*. I am telling you this so that in case these gentlemen turn up abroad, asking for assistance or recommendations to go and serve as pilots in the Soviet Union, you will know how to treat them.

Dirty swine! Luckily, on Friday, the situation at Albacete having improved a little, we managed to establish regular contact with Martínez and the local organization....

...That's all so far as our personal vicissitudes are concerned. And now something about the situation in the country and the perspective in which we are working, which is not so bad as might be imagined. The establishment of the junta and the flight of N. [Negrín] and his government (this flight, in my view, was a tragic mistake and quite inexplicable; I end up suspecting N. of complicity with Casado: your relations with N. outside the country, your statements concerning him, etc. will have to be very careful) have created an extremely serious situation in the country, of confusion, disorder and something resembling 18 July† – with the aggravating difference of a brutal repression unleashed against our p. This repression was ordered by the junta from above, with the manifest intention of thus making an agreement with Franco possible, and was fed at the base by an explosion of all the hatred for our party and spirit of revenge of anarchists, provocateurs, etc., etc. The plan was to shatter our p. and in effect suppress it. The p. was surprised by this wave of repression, which moreover highlighted our weaknesses, especially in relation to our links with the masses. There is no organization of the p. – so far as I know – that had the capacity to defend itself by posing the problem of defence of the p. as a mass problem. The majority took the course of utilizing "positions" of the p. within the army and the civilian apparatus of the State, but a considerable proportion of the men holding such "positions" failed us (the airmen, for example, accepted Casado's orders to bomb the lines occupied by our comrades in Madrid). So far as the masses are concerned, in the first days at least the anti-communist campaign chalked up some successes, thanks to the profound weariness of the masses themselves, who desired peace above all else and to whom the p. had

---

* The so-called National Defence Council established by the republican officers who, in March 1939, rose against the Negrín government. Led by Segismundo Casado López, a colonel in the republican army, they favoured negotiations with Franco and eliminated communists from positions of power.

† The day in 1936 when the military rising began in mainland Spain.

been presented as the enemy of peace, responsible for a new civil war. In Madrid the comrades were provoked to armed struggle by the junta's measures, the arrests and summary executions of our command staff and commissars, etc. etc. Moreover, they thought the government was resisting elsewhere in the country. I do not yet know all the details, but it seems to me that once the decision was taken to defend ourselves by every means, our comrades lacked decision. Their sense of responsibility, undoubtedly, prevented them from calling extra forces into the capital, with the risk of breaching the fronts....

Report of May 21, 1939[5]

Strictly confidential

The difficulties which the resistance and unity policy of the Spanish party has come up against have begun to increase and intensify, especially since the Munich capitulation, and since the general strike and rupture of the popular front in France.* The information and comments that follow relate to the period intervening between these events and the end of the war. If the report has a somewhat too descriptive character, that is due to the need to furnish as much material as possible on the facts regarding a period of the war about which, until the present time, I have not been able to send you any information....

...*Last attempts at political action.* On March 11 (Saturday) Checa and I finally managed to meet up with Jesús and the other leaders from the east, in Jesús's command post in the mountains near Valencia. We studied the situation, and all came to the conclusion there was nothing more to be done on the path of armed struggle, but that there was still some minimal possibility of altering the situation in our favour, by basing ourselves on a number of elements who, though they had helped the junta in the first few days, were now dissatisfied; realized that they had made an idiotic blunder, since Casado did not have peace all wrapped up as he had given them to understand; and above all wished to go back to collaborating with the communist party. We decided to test this possibility. Among these elements were: General Menéndez, Commander-in-Chief of the whole army;† the republican Just, from Valencia; the socialist Rodríguez Vega. Menéndez stated that he did not want to rebel against the junta, but he let it be understood that, if we brought Miaja to Valencia,‡ it would be possible to organize a political action against Casado. We tried to do this, but Casado scented the danger and prevented Miaja from leaving Madrid.

---

[5] This report was in fact written after Togliatti's return to Moscow.

* The last Blum government in France saw the inexorable fragmentation of the "left bloc" and violent repression of the November 1938 general strike. [*Footnote from the Italian text*]

† Leopoldo Menéndez López, republican general commanding the army of the East in the final period of the war. [*Footnote from the Italian text*]

‡ José Miaja Menant, republican army general, played an important role in the defence of Madrid; subsequently commander of the centre-south front and then inspector-general

The contacts with Menéndez and Just to try and alter the situation lasted several days. But the perspective (or illusion) that we still possessed vanished completely after Menéndez's trip to Madrid, around March 15. It was the socialist Carrillo,* in league with the most virulent anti-communists of the whole country and on Casado's direct orders, who managed to gain control of the situation and made Menéndez pull back, threatening him with dismissal. But this final attempt at political action brought us many positive consequences. First, protected as we were in Valencia by Menéndez himself, it allowed us to work a bit more freely and link up with almost all the base organizations, the better to organize evacuation of our cadres. Secondly, it allowed us to avoid our soldiers being expelled from the army and at once arrested everywhere: Menéndez refused to do that. Thirdly, it was possible to avoid expulsion of the communists from the UGT: during a meeting of the UGT leadership held in Valencia (on the 15 or 16), Vega made a bloc for this purpose with our comrades, against the Caballerists who were calling for expulsion. Fourthly, it allowed us to utilize a few legal possibilities for evacuating our cadres. Fifthly, it allowed us to carry out a real mass distribution of the party manifesto drafted between the 16 and 17, which contained a complete historical and political assessment of the situation in which the war was drawing to a close. And finally, it allowed us to retain important and very useful positions at Cartagena till the very end.

The party's base organizations did not respond well during this last period. Isolated from the masses, expelled from the popular front, town councils and everywhere, the comrades were very fearful of any action or statement. In the practical work, the abrupt change in the situation had disoriented almost everyone. Accustomed to power and the possibilities for action that this offered, they were no longer able to act swiftly in a situation of semi-illegality. It is necessary to signal as a splendid exception the energetic attitude of one comrade, a member of the municipal council of Valencia, who denounced Casado's treachery with extraordinary vigour in the council chamber. He was thrown into prison, and I do not know where he is now. In Valencia, following the orders received, we established a new party leadership made up of the following comrades: Larrañaga, Rosas, Sosa, Navarro Ballesteros, Montolín, Pinto, a youth leader. During the last few days we worked with this new leadership.

Around 20 March, when this new leadership had already organized its work, we received a message to go to Cartagena where there was a possibility of getting out. Jesús was already on the spot. When we arrived (during the night of 21 March) we discovered that this possibility did not exist, and on the morning of 24 March we were obliged to seize an airfield and three planes by force. Having left Totana (Cartagena) at six, we landed at about ten in Mostaganem (Algeria). With me were Jesús Hernández, Checa, Diéguez, Uribes, Palau, Virgilio Llanos, etc. . . .

---

of the armed forces, he finally became president of Casado's National Defence Council. [*Footnote from the Italian text*]

* Wenceslao Carrillo, a leader of the PSOE, took part in the coup organized by Casado to overthrow the Negrín government. Father of Santiago Carrillo, future leader of the PCE. [*Footnote from the Italian text*]

INDEX

Adler, F., 48, 65, 72, 89–90
agriculture, 33, 56
Albacete, 37, 58, 77–8, 98; conference (April 1937), 40
Alcalá Zamora, N., 8
Alicante, 75, 98
Almería, 48, 61, 74
Alonso, B., 99
Álvarez del Vayo, J.: as commissar-general, 22; subservience to Soviet advice, 38n8; at 1937 Albacete conference, 40; loses Foreign Ministry, 42; resigns as head of commissariat, 63–4; reappointed to government, 68; accepts defeat, 74–5
Amsterdam International, 13, 46–9, 69
Ananios, 99
anarchists: in 1936 elections, 3; differences with socialists, 11; decline to join Largo Caballero's government, 15, 31; fighting formations and militias, 31, 57; relations with PCE, 32–5, 54, 56; arrested and persecuted, 36; in 1937 Barcelona rising, 40, 54; Togliatti on, 55, 93, 96–7; and peasant collectives, 56; see also Confederación Nacional del Trabajo; Federación Anarquista Ibérica
Angell, Sir Norman, 82
Annemasse conference (June 1937), 48–9, 52, 64, 89–90
Antonov-Ovseenko, V., 22, 33
Aragon, 1, 35, 55–7, 61
Araquistáin, L., 34n44, 38n8, 42n16
army (republican): reorganised, 29, 45, 57–8; strength, 58; PCE infiltration, 58–9; PCE demand reform of, 66

Asturias, 6, 11, 21, 61
Attlee, C., 75n35
Austria, 67
Azaña, M.: enthusiasm for popular front, 1; 1936 government, 8; and French sympathy, 13; leaves Madrid for Barcelona, 27, 32; and Largo Caballero's resignation, 42; defensive attitude, 46; and German bombardment of Almería, 48; proposes peace overtures, 66; retires to Paris, 75; Stalin on, 87

Bank of Spain, 26
Barcelona: loyalty to republic, 11; Soviet Consul-General in, 22; united front in, 31–2; May 1937 rising, 40–1, 43, 54; government transferred to, 61–2, 69; moves to defection, 63; situation in, 69–70; food shortages, 71; churches reopened, 72; nationalist offensive and capture of, 73–4; see also Catalonia
Basques, Basque region, 5, 21, 38–9
Batalla, La (journal), 6, 41, 43
Berzin, Gen. J. P., 32
Besteiro, J., 1, 72, 76
Bevin, E., 47
Bibolotti, A., 52
Bilbao, 38, 60
Bloque Popular see popular front
Blükher, Marshal V. K., 51n21
Blum, L., 12, 14, 46n3, 100n
Bonté, F., 49n11
Britain: attitude to Spanish situation, 13–14, 50, 64, 75n35; and non-intervention, 16–18, 23; benign Soviet attitude to 28; proposes settlement to republicans, 67, 69; Polish treaty, 81

ABOUT THE AUTHOR

Edward Hallett Carr was born in 1892 and educated at Merchant Taylors' School, London, and Trinity College, Cambridge. After joining the Foreign Office (1916) to work in Paris and Riga, he was appointed Assistant Adviser on League of Nations Affairs, First Secretary in the Foreign Office and, for one year during World War II, Director of Foreign Publicity at the Ministry of Information in London. From 1941 to 1946, he served simultaneously as Wilson Professor of International Politics at the University College of Wales and as Assistant Editor for *The Times*, eventually settling in Oxford as a Fellow at Trinity College in Cambridge.

In November of 1982, E.H. Carr died in Cambridge. He was at work on this book, which was to be part of his *History of Soviet Russia*.

Praise for Twilight of the Comintern

"Undoubtedly the most thorough and satisfactory reconstruction of a tangled tale."
—*The New York Times Book Review*

"An indispensable continuation of Carr's multi-volume *History of Soviet Russia*, one of the great historical projects of this century....Carr brings the whole business to life."
—*Kirkus*

"This is an account both dense and detailed and one that presents an exceptional analysis of the issues, strategies, and personalities involved on this struggle and debate on the future of communism." —*Booklist*

"A fitting conclusion to the *History of Soviet Russia*, which established Carr not only as the towering giant among Western specialists of recent Russian history but certainly also as the leading British historian of his generation."—Arno Mayer